The Sexual Citizen

The Sexual Citizen

Queer Politics and Beyond

David Bell and Jon Binnie

Polity

First published in 2000 by Polity Press in association with Blackwell Publishers Ltd

Editorial office:
Polity Press
65 Bridge Street
Cambridge CB2 1UR, UK

Marketing and production:
Blackwell Publishers Ltd
108 Cowley Road
Oxford OX4 1JF, UK

Published in the USA by
Blackwell Publishers Inc.
Commerce Place
350 Main Street
Malden, MA 02148, USA

Library of Congress Cataloging-in-Publication Data

Bell, David.
    The sexual citizen : queer theory and beyond / David Bell and Jon Binnie.
        p. cm.
    Includes bibliographical references and index.
    ISBN 0-7456-1653-4—ISBN 0-7456-1654-2 (pbk.)
        1. Homosexuality—Political aspects. 2. Lesbianism—Political aspects. 3. Sex role—Political aspects. 4. Gender identity—Political aspects. 5. Citizenship. I. Binnie, Jon. II. Title.

HQ76.25.B45 2000
306.76'6—dc21

00–039971

A catalogue record for this book is available from the British Library.

Typeset in 11 on 13 pt Photina
by Kolam Information Services Private Limited, Pondicherry, India
Printed in Great Britain by MPG Books Ltd, Bodmin, Cornwall

This book is printed on acid-free paper.

Contents

Acknowledgements

We should like to thank the following people for their help, support and encouragement during the writing of this book: Jo Eadie, Ruth Holliday, Kath Moonan, Bev Skeggs. At Polity Press, Rebecca Harkin has been a supportive and patient editor, and we thank her too as well as Sue Leigh who saw us through the final stages.

1

Sexing Citizenship

The time has come to think about queering the state.
Lisa Duggan, 'Queering the state'

Something strange has happened to citizenship.
Lauren Berlant, The Queen of America Goes to Washington City

The re-emergence of questions of citizenship in the UK and the USA in the 1980s, and subsequent political and academic debates around those questions, form a useful backdrop for thinking about the changing forms and uses of sexual politics. In this book, we seek to explore some aspects of what has come to be called *sexual citizenship*, located against that backdrop but also moving beyond it. By focusing on particular facets of sexual citizenship – the role of the market, the city as a site of citizenship, the place of notions of love, family and the social, the globalization of sexual identities and politics – we attempt to broaden the terms of the debate, as well as offering an assessment of the usefulness of continuing to view sexualities through the lens of citizenship. After two decades of debate – not just in the academy, but in law courts and state offices, and on the streets – we feel that the time has come to reflect on the question of sexual citizenship; to ask, *was it worth it?* What have we learnt from the debates, where are we now, where do we go from here?

The task of thinking about sexual citizenship, in fact, is one that has attracted considerable interest among academics and activists. As the notion of citizenship re-entered political, academic and

popular discourses in the 1980s – spurred on, in the UK, by the
Conservative administration's notions of active citizenship, of a
Citizen's Charter, and of emphasizing the flipsides of the equation
of citizenship (rights *always* come with responsibilities), as well as
by a brief flurry of excitement over communitarianism – so it
entered the register of sexual politics. With its mobile combinations
of the political, the economic, the social, the legal and the ethical,
citizenship seemed to be a neat concept for articulating (and agitat-
ing) the field of sexual politics generally.

It is the purpose of this introductory chapter to establish the
terrain for the argument that runs through *The Sexual Citizen*.
There are a lot of issues to deal with, in terms of laying out the
current articulations of the notion of citizenship, as well as sketch-
ing the current climate of sexual politics. We can then intertwine
these two threads by looking at the figure of the sexual citizen: who
is he or she, and how does he or she enact sexual citizenship? What
projects is the sexual citizen engaged in? Inevitably, such questions
call for definitions, and for the telling of a number of stories –
political stories, sexual stories, economic stories, social and cultural
stories. To understand the sexual citizen, then, we need to understand the conditions that give rise to the possibility (even, we might
argue, the necessity) of such a figure. That is the prime directive of
this chapter, for it frames the subsequent discussions of the book.
Before that, however, it is important to establish the logic of the
trajectory that *The Sexual Citizen* takes in order to explore these
questions. If we sketch our argument here, we can then begin the
task of unpacking it, of laying out the terms and conditions that will
engage us through the remaining chapters.

Our story of sexual citizenship is an ambivalent one. While we
recognize the political potency of mobilizing (maybe even colon-
izing) the notion of citizenship with an agenda of sexual politics, we
are concerned with the limitations as well as the opportunities this
strategy affords. In order to make this ambivalence manifest, we
have chosen to settle on key sites of the sexual citizenship debate;
sites that we hope will illustrate precisely that tension between
opportunity and limitation. For us, many of the current nodes of
the political articulation of sexual citizenship are marked by compromise; this is inherent in the very notion itself, as we have already
noted: the twinning of rights with responsibilities in the logic of

citizenship is another way of expressing compromise – *we will grant you certain rights if (and only if) you match these by taking on certain responsibilities*. Every entitlement is freighted with a duty. In our reading of sexual politics, rights claims articulated through appeals to citizenship carry the burden of compromise in particular ways; this demands the circumscription of 'acceptable' modes of being a sexual citizen. This is, of course, an age-old compromise that sexual dissidents have long had to negotiate; the current problem is its cementing into rights-based political strategies, which forecloses or denies aspects of sexuality written off as 'unacceptable'. In particular, given the current political climate, this tends to demand a modality of sexual citizenship that is privatized, deradicalized, de-eroticized and *confined* in all senses of the word: kept in place, policed, limited. Jeffrey Weeks (1999, p. 37) argues that the 'moment of citizenship' represents the only way that 'difference can [ever] find a proper home' – we think that is an especially telling phrase: who defines what a 'proper home' is for sexual citizens? What happens to those who refuse to be confined to 'home', or to living in the 'proper' way? We will return to Weeks' argument later in this chapter, since it represents a particular take on sexual citizenship that we must engage with.

In order to explore the project of sexual citizenship, we have chosen to focus on a number of different domains. While these are not meant to be exhaustive, we think that each serves to illustrate the workings of the debate around sexual citizenship in particularly illuminating ways. In chapter 3, for example, our focus is on two key articulations of sexual-citizenship rights: the claiming of the right to 'marriage' and the claiming of the right to join the armed forces. The shape of these rights claims gives us an insight into the mechanisms that frame sexual citizenship in the field of law and politics; moreover, the logic which gives that frame its intelligibility and legitimacy as the basis for demanding equality of citizenship opens up the questions that lie at the heart of this book: what form are claims for sexual citizenship made to take in the legal-political context of late-modern liberal democracies? What agendas are forged in such rights claims? And how are those agendas negotiated in the spaces of law and politics?

The introduction of space into our discussion is, in fact, crucial. As Engin Isin and Patricia Wood (1999, p. viii) note in their recent book *Citizenship and Identity*, arguments about citizenship must include a 'recognition of the relevance of space, that is, the locations from which people exercise their citizenship rights'. This notion informs a number of the domains we discuss in *The Sexual Citizen*: we consider the space of the social, the space of the city and transnational space as different locations from which people exercise their (sexual) citizenship rights. Each is, in its own way, a space of sexual citizenship. In the case of the social, for example, we have to consider the field of social action as one in which the enunciation of sexual identity-positions occurs, but also as a space in which the limitations of those identity-positions are especially manifest. Similarly, we want to explore arguments about the relationship between sexual identity (and especially homosexual identity) and urban space: if the city is the stage on which homosexuality is enacted, what are the implications for sexual citizenship of current reshapings of the urban environment, driven by political imperatives often inflected by a distinct agenda? Sometimes this involves the marketing of cities as democratic sites of diversity and difference, while in other contexts it involves the 'cleaning up' of a city's image through red-lining sexual subcultures into marginal spaces, producing what is effectively a moral topography of sexual citizenship – gentrified housing is good, spaces of consumption are okay, but sites of public sex, sex work and pornography are bad.

Further, given the historical equation of citizenship with the public sphere, the reprivatization of public space in the contemporary city has severe repercussions for sexual citizens. In fact, the public/private divide is perhaps the most fundamental spatiality of sexual citizenship, articulated in diverse ways throughout this book. Jeffrey Weeks (1999, p. 37) again marks this vector of sexual citizenship ambivalently: 'The sexual citizen...makes a claim to transcend the limits of the personal sphere by going public, but the going public is, in a necessary but nevertheless paradoxical move, about protecting the possibilities of private life and private choice in a more inclusive society.' The outcome of rights claims, then, is to secure *private* space to be a sexual citizen; while this might involve an intervention into the public sphere (what Weeks names 'the moment of transgression'), this is merely a tactic to enable the claim to privacy – the 'proper home' of the sexual citizen. From our perspective, such a programme is intensely problematic, not least because it sides with phobic arguments that grant sexual rights only on the understanding that they will be kept private: that is, invisible (Cooper, 1993a). While there is a need to protect some notion of privacy – if that means defining a space where law cannot intervene, for example – there is a bigger risk to be taken in stressing the private as the proper home of sexual citizenship (Bell, 1995a, 1995b). Part of that risk, which is also manifest in the agitations for the legalization of lesbian and gay 'marriage', is that it restates the family as the private site of citizenship. In current sexual rights claims, the struggle to define 'families we choose' bears the mark of this privatization impulse, as if the retreat into family-space is a necessary strategy for claiming citizen status – something that closes down ways of living and loving that don't accord with the model of the family, no matter how it is expanded. In fact, the motif of family returns again and again in our analysis, reflecting Elspeth Probyn's (1998, p. 170) assertion that 'the widespread familialization of the social and the currency of the familial citizen is rearranging the very contours of the social surface. It is thus crucial that we carefully study the mutations of the lines that are composing the familial citizen' – one of the most significant mutations being the shifting balance between public and private spheres. Sexual citizenship performs an uneasy negotiation of the public/private split, then – something that we shall return to throughout *The Sexual Citizen*.

At a different scale, we must also consider the transnational spaces of sexual citizenship. Here, in the wake of globalization's disjunctive flows of people, ideas and images (Appadurai, 1996), we are faced with a radical transformation in the logics of citizenship, traditionally predicated on a sense of belonging rooted in the nation-state (Stychin, 1998). Instances in the politics of transnational sexual citizenship, such as the 'Europeanization' of human rights law, the regulation of immigration policies or the globalizing of sexual identities, ask that we re-evaluate the boundaries of sexual citizenship and rights claims in recognition of the changing shape of the world.

Aside from these scales of sexual citizenship, there are other transformations that have profoundly impacted on how and where the sexual citizen is constituted as a culturally legible figure. In the current debates on citizenship more broadly, one dimension that has attracted close scrutiny is the role of the market in recasting the working of citizenship. In the politics of the UK's Citizen's Charter and the rhetoric of active citizenship – which, despite its new right origins, lingers on in centre-left discourses – there is an inevitable marketization of rights; the citizen is made over as a particular kind of sovereign consumer, who has the right to choose and 'buy' access to aspects of collective consumption provided traditionally by the state (welfare, health care, education). As we have already noted, the market has indeed created new spaces of sexual citizenship, in the form of visible spaces of consumption – so-called gay villages. This introduces us to an argument that has been central to certain trajectories of rights agitation in the domain of lesbian and gay politics in recent years: that the commercial presence and power of gay men and lesbians – short-handed as the 'pink economy' – makes a strong foundation on which to base rights claims, given the marketized logic that links economic power to political power. Consumer citizens voice their politics through their spending, and can therefore make rights claims as *consumers* (Gabriel and Lang, 1995). There are very real dangers in this argument, however, not least that the myth of the pink economy serves to deny both economic inequalities between sexual citizens and the economic limitations (in terms, for example, of employment opportunities) that act as a further limit on the enactment of sexual citizenship. The orientation of the sexual citizen to the seductions and dangers of the market marks another key ambivalence, which we explore in more detail in chapter 6.

What we have been trying to do so far, then, is to move towards a moment of defining sexual citizenship. We have sketched some of the sites where the sexual citizen appears in various guises, but we have yet to tackle head-on the question of definition. In order to move closer to that moment, we need to begin with the notion of citizenship itself, in order to survey the discourses within which sexual citizenship gets articulated.

Thinking and rethinking citizenship

We do not propose to provide here a thoroughgoing analysis of theoretical material on citizenship, since there seems little merit in retreading ground already compacted by the feet of so many before us; we'd rather cut to the chase. We do, however, want to offer some pointers, some snapshots of the ways in which citizenship has been approached as a useful and usable political discourse or thematic. We offer little more, then, than a reading list of citizenship texts and authors, since our concern is more squarely with the workings of the logic of citizenship in the particular context of sexual identities and politics.

The particular starting point for understandings of the modern condition of citizenship is the work of T. H. Marshall, especially his 1950 essay *Citizenship and Social Class* (reprinted 1973). Revisions, critiques and extensions of Marshall's theorizing have filled many pages (e.g. Turner, 1990, 1993). The civic liberalist tradition in citizenship theory is most closely aligned to Marshall, with its analysis of the state's paternal role in securing the welfare and rights of its citizens, as well as binding citizens together in sociality. The second major strand of 'modern' citizenship thinking, civic republicanism (in which we can include communitarianism), places more stress on obligation, often mediated through political participation in common affairs. The nation-state is placed centre-stage in civic republicanist conceptions of citizenship, as is national identity. The contemporary citizenship debate has, however, moved a long way beyond Marshall, thanks mainly to feminist and post-structuralist rereadings of the terms and conditions of being a citizen, which place stress on questions of *difference* (Mouffe, 1993; Phillips, 1993; Young, 1989). Simultaneously, the question of *where* one is a citizen of has been necessarily addressed in the wake of transnational and global forms of both politics and belonging (Isin and Wood, 1999).

Pluralist, feminist and poststructuralist takes on citizenship have become fashionable in the academy, chiming as they do with the reinvention of politics under postmodernity (Yeatman, 1994). Most commentators assert that there is something within the notion of citizenship that can further a radical democratic project, despite recuperation by new right politicians – mobilized in the UK, for example, around the figure of the active citizen and in the drafting of a Citizen's Charter (Cooper, 1993b; Kearns, 1992; Ignatieff, 1991), and in the USA through neoconservative discourses around welfare and the family (Roche, 1992). By adding in insights from poststructuralist theory – most notably those that concern the 'decentring' of the subject, and which therefore raise questions about *identity* itself – such approaches seek to complicate (and simultaneously re-energize) the figure of the citizen and its relation to forms of identity politics. As Anne Phillips (1993, p. 87) writes: [t]he value of citizenship lies in the way it restates the importance of politicial activity... [T]his might prove itself as a way of dealing with the politics of an extraordinary time.' Reflecting the poststructuralist perspective, this 'extraordinary time' is described in Paul Clarke's *Deep Citizenship* (1996, p. 116) as one of transformation: 'the world into which we are moving is fractured in multiple ways,... its meta-narratives have collapsed,... its old ideologies have fallen into disrepute and... its old certainties have been transformed into new uncertainties'.

That sense of fragmentation, of new uncertainties, certainly provides one of the motor mechanisms for restating citizenship in political discourse. It also affords the opportunity to radically rethink what being a citizen is all about; shifting the boundaries, then, of a particular form of political identity. Such a shift has been widely remarked upon. Anthony Giddens, for example, talks of a move towards 'life politics' in *Modernity and Self-Identity* (1991). Important political movements in the West – feminism, civil rights, gay liberation, student protests, new social movements, 'body politics' – can be taken to indicate this transition, especially when coupled with Giddens' assertion of the increasing reflexivity of (post)modern life. Traces of this shift can be noted in poststructuralist readings of citizenship, and in related rewritings, such as Paul Clarke's work on 'deep citizenship'. Clarke (1996, p. 118) writes that 'the practice of the virtues and the development of deep citizenship cannot be separated from the development of selfhood'; indeed, deep citizenship brings together 'care of the self, care of others and care of the world'. Crucially for Clarke, '[t]o be a deep citizen is to determine for oneself that an action is political' (p. 125) – reflexive life politics, then.

Nick Ellison (1997, p. 711), however, offers a somewhat different conception of the condition he names 'reflexive citizenship'. For Ellison, reflexivity means 'the general process, driven by social, political and economic change, by which social actors, confronted with the erosion, or transformation, of established patterns of belonging, readjust existing notions of rights and membership to new conceptions of identity, solidarity and the institutional foci of redress'. Ellison disputes Giddens' focus on individualization and voluntarism, however, asserting citizenship as a *defensive* strategy – a way of trying to retain a sense of integration in an increasingly complex world. Ellison offers a cautious, indeed at times pessimistic, reading of the reflexive turn, since the ability to mobilize reflexive citizenship is not equally distributed in society, suggesting that some marginalized groups are effectively denied the right to act politically as citizens, and may have no choice but to elect for disengagement instead, thereby ushering in a revival of the 'classical' notion of citizenship as a marker of social and political privilege. Whether or not we are to side with Ellison's cautionary tale, or subscribe instead to Giddens' upbeat mode of reflexive life politics, it remains clear that the very notion of citizenship, while endlessly deconstructed and reconstructed, serves as a useful device for thinking about forms of political action and political identity. We shall revisit this aspect of the rewriting of citizenship later, in the context of attempts to put Giddens' thesis to use in arguments about the sexual citizen.

Ellison's assessment raises an important question, then, about how citizens are engaged in politics – and about what we mean by *the politics of citizenship* itself. A useful critical summary of the roles available to citizens in the current polity is offered by Holloway Sparks (1997), in an essay on 'dissident citizenship'. Sparks argues that the political role of citizens within current citizenship theory is both limited and limiting, and suggests the need to expand our conception of citizenship to incorporate dissent. She argues that dissent has 'fallen through the cracks of much mainstream citizenship theory', which has instead focused on attempts to secure rights within the public sphere of advanced captialist market societies (p.77). This theorization advances a model of 'participatory democracy', Sparks argues, that sidelines dissent as a political practice. The roles for citizens within participatory democracy cannot always accomodate such dissident modes of politics, which Sparks defines as 'the public contestation of prevailing arrangements of power by marginalized citizens through oppositional, democratic, noninstitutionalized practices that augment or replace institutionalized channels of democratic opposition when those channels are inadequate or unavailable' (p. 83).

Sparks makes use of Nancy Fraser's notion of 'subaltern counter-publics' in her theorization of dissident citizenship. Such spaces are defined by Fraser (1992, p. 123) as 'parallel discursive areas where members of subordinate groups invent and circulate counterdiscourses to formulate oppositional interpretations of their identities, interests, and needs'. Importantly, Sparks concludes that her revisioning of citizenship is valuable in that it suggests we must acknowledge that dissident politics is still the *politics of citizens*, as well as broadening our definition of where politics takes place. That these concepts have clear resonances with the kinds of politics mobilized by *sexual* dissidents will become clear later. With this in mind, we shall now turn our attention to attempts to mobilize the concept of citizenship specifically within the context of sexuality, offering a brief but critical reading of a number of key texts.

Sexing citizenship

Central to our thinking, as will become clear, is the notion that *all citizenship is sexual citizenship*, in that the foundational tenets of being a citizen are all inflected by sexualities. Indeed, many of the ways in which citizenship discourses operate can be read as discourses around the 'sexing' of citizens – for example, the centring of notions of the family obviously draws on sexualized constructions of appropriate (and inappropriate) modes of living together and caring for one another. Feminist critiques of the gendered assumptions inherent in the very term 'family' can therefore be supplemented by, for example, interrogating the assumptions contained in the rhetoric of the British new right around 'pretended families' (Weeks, 1991). Similarly, as we shall see, the bonds of citizenship are in a sense bonds of love – Clarke's call for 'care of the self, care of others and care of the world' speaks to this kind of citizen-love. But, as Freud (1921) argued, this happy, cohesive homosociality relies on the denial or prohibition of the homosexual, whose eroticizing of the social bond threatens its collapse. Contemporary moments in the reinscription of modes of citizenship – the military exclusion policy, for example – illustrate the continued policing of these institutionalized homosocial/homosexual boundaries. Further, 'family' and 'love' are brought together in questions of marriage; as we shall see in chapter 3, appeals for legislative change around same-sex marriage also bring to the surface issues of sexual citizenship – of rights, of duties, of politics and of identities.

The question of thinking sexual citizenship can be (and indeed has been) approached from many different perspectives. Work in legal theory, in political theory, in sociology and beyond evidences the manysidedness of citizenship. Is 'citizen' a legal category, a political category or a sociological category? The simple answer is that it is all of these – and many other things, too. Again, we do not propose here a comprehensive list of texts where the concept of sexual citizenship is constructed (or critiqued). We offer instead a meditation on selected texts that approach the question in distinct ways, with different agendas and perspectives. Some of these texts we have previously turned our critical attentions to (Bell, 1997; Binnie, 1998), while in subsequent chapters we further engage with the question of sexual citizenship through a reading of select current debates and incidents. Setting a broad agenda for considering sexual citizenship, Steven Seidman writes:

> Citizenship rights make it possible for individuals to protect themselves against social threat, to participate in public decision-making, to make claims about national policy and culture, and so on. At stake is how the lesbian and gay movement approach [*sic*] questions of citizenship. Contestation should be over the basis of citizenship and the meaning of sexual and intimate citizenship. In short, we need a queer articulation of democratic theory.   (1998, p. 189)

We shall begin to attend to this agenda not at the beginning (if indeed such a thing could be located), but with a text that nonetheless bills itself on its jacket as 'the first book to approach sexuality from the perspective of citizenship' – David Evans' *Sexual Citizenship* (1993). Evans' principal concern is with what he calls the 'material construction' of sexual citizenship, and to theorize this he explores in detail the interplay of the state and the market. Reading citizenship under capitalism as the mediation of these two spheres leads Evans to consider the commodification of sexuality; his foregrounding of a notion of 'consumer citizenship' is a consequence of the political climate in the UK at the time he was

writing (although much of the substance of this remains today): the
citizen is a taxpayer and a consumer existing in the context of a free
market and a non-interventionist state – a situation embodied for
Evans in the Citizen's Charter introduced by the Major administration in 1991 (see also Cooper, 1993b). Facilitating this mode of
citizenship requires the splitting of legality from morality, so that
rights may be granted in law while still being subject to the moralizing gaze (such a distinction, for Evans, is central to post-
Wolfenden sexual citizenship in the UK, and hangs upon a notion
of distinct public and private realms, effectively policing 'public
morality' and thereby 'privatizing' sexualities deemed 'immoral').
The sum of this, in Evans' words, is to define sexual citizenship as a
matter of 'partial, private, and primarily leisure and lifestyle membership' (p. 64). In subsequent chapters, he then counterposes
'economic rights' with 'political obligations' as the flipsides of
'homosexual citizenship'.

Continuing his argument, Evans describes the then current situation of 'male homosexual citizenship' in the UK thus:

> Male homosexual citizenship is predicated on the conjunction of
> individual consenting adult freedoms including, indeed particularly,
> those of a consuming market, and the reinforced stigma of immor-
> ality which bans this citizen from the 'moral community' and polices
> him into privacy. As gay men claimed their leisure and lifestyle
> market, the market claimed them, colonised and exploited gay sex-
> uality.   (p. 100)

This leads Evans into a discussion of the (economic) 'virilisation' of
gay men, and thence through a somewhat squeamish and voyeur-
istic litany of the commercial gay scene's many 'sexual markets'.
Against this mode of consumer citizenship, he sets politico-legal
issues of 'citizenship conflict': legal status, law enforcement and
policing, censorship, media representation, employment rights,
sex education and Section 28's ban on the 'promotion of homosexuality' (to which Evans gives most attention). Overshadowing all
of these is the AIDS epidemic, which has been central to redefini-
tions of sexual citizenship. A similar shadow is inevitably cast by
the authoritarian populism and nostalgic familial moralizing of
Thatcherism and its lasting legacy.

The key trope, then, of *Sexual Citizenship* is of the negotiations between state and market in relation to formations of sexual identity and community. Evans expands his gaze to consider bisexual and transgender issues, as well as the constructions of children as sexual objects and sexual subjects, and 'female sexual citizenship', exploring in each case legal, political and moral issues, always alongside questions of commodification – for if Evans' book is about any one thing, then it is about the reduction of sexuality to a commodity form, through the marketization of 'identity' as 'lifestyle'.

A very different notion of sexual citizenship is mobilized in Davina Cooper's *Power in Struggle* (1995). Centred around a critical Foucauldian-feminist analysis of the functioning of state power, Cooper's text provides us with a sense of 'relational power' – polysemic, shape-shifting, metamorphic. Into this network of power, then, forms of resistance cannot be read as being straightforwardly oppositional. To explore the implications of this formulation, Cooper reads through discourses of and around sex radicalism, lesbian parenting, and lesbian and gay involvement in local state politics. Through these three quite different terrains, Cooper is able to consider particular strategies for 'sexing the state'.

In her discussion of sexual transgression as a political tactic, Cooper follows an increasingly common line that critiques transgressive acts. She describes such acts as 'strategies which focus on the power of sex and bodies as a means of engineering change', chiefly mobilized by 'a narrow range of people, principally young, middle-class, white lesbians and gay men within a limited range of sociopolitical and cultural arenas', and as having a focus on sexuality 'as a discrete social practice or relationship rather than on the ways in which institutionalized terrains such as the criminal justice process, welfare provision and education are themselves sexualized' (p. 54). This limits their broader political reach, Cooper argues, reprivatizing sexuality in terms of personal freedom – an argument we would certainly take issue with.

Cooper's reading of the brief moral panic in the UK in 1991 over so-called virgin births offers a window into the notion of relational (or productive) power, since the furore created by tabloid sensationalism around lesbian motherhood had contradictory effects: it was seized by the new right to justify tightening controls on access to assisted conception technologies, and became a centrepiece for the more broad-reaching anxieties circulating around the 'crisis of the family', reinstating a naturalized discourse of 'penetrative procreation'. At the same time, though, it brought donor insemination on to mainstream agendas – appearing on talk shows, even in sitcom plots – giving previously invisible lesbian mothers a discursive presence that could now be talked about. By closely reading the complex negotiations within governing agencies, Cooper complexifies the picture of state interventions into such discursive presences, suggesting constant flux in the midst of attempts to fix meaning.

Similarly, her reading of entryism – via lesbian and gay presence in British local (municipal) politics – teases out the problematics of working for change *within* the state apparatus (this material is more fully covered in her 1994 book *Sexing the City*). Within some British metropolitan left-wing councils, lesbian and gay politics achieved a certain kind of power in the early 1980s, which itself became the subject of a right-wing backlash (Section 28 was in large part an attack on pro-gay initiatives in 'Loony Left' councils). Such moves also faced opposition for 'desexualizing' homosexuality precisely by pushing it into a social policy context – municipal activism, as Cooper names it, became synonymous with incorporation (as well as with 'professionalization', with *using* state power rather than seeking to *oppose* it; a similar tension is discussed in relation to the AIDS 'shadow state' by Brown (1997)). This is, then, the core of Cooper's position on the uses and effects of power: that no one strategy can be adopted as fit for all occasions, and that what is required is instead a 'strategic pluralism' (1995, p. 125) that can match the polymorphousness of state power. At particular times, in particular contexts, entryist strategies may be the most effective, while in others more oppositional or confrontational tactics may serve political ends better. Cooper's formulation, ultimately, is of a shifting portfolio of responses – counterhegemony, antihegemony and radical hegemony – which all have their part to play. Such a position relies on what she calls generosity, which she defines as 'the recognition that strategies and struggles may prove beneficial (within certain time-frames and junctures) even if they are not the ones we ourselves might choose' (p. 135).

Such a pluralized notion of resistance takes us back to Cooper's conceptualization of 'state sexualisation', wherein the state itself must be de-essentialized as a 'contingently articulated, multifaceted phenomenon with no fixed form, essence or core' (pp. 60–1), with the implication that relations between the state and questions of sexuality are equally proliferate and equally contingent – the state has interests in mobilizing certain notions of sexuality, but may also consequently and inadvertently mobilize others, as Cooper's work on donor insemination shows. The contrast between Cooper's finely textured (though not unproblematic) rendering of sexual citizenship and David Evans' should, then, be clear: Evans leaves the state relatively uninterrogated, and certainly constructs it in monolithic terms, allowing no real space for dissidence outside the market; his notion of oppositional politics further lacks the nuances of Cooper's strategic pluralism.

A similarly complex picture, though with a somewhat different agenda to *Power in Struggle*, is found in Lisa Duggan's provocative essay 'Queering the state' (1995), which is grounded in US-based struggles over sexual citizenship. Duggan paints an equally contingent and pluralized picture of state power and of competing discourses around sexuality (for instance, by naturalizing heterosexuality while rendering homosexuality 'contagious', as in 'No Promo Homo' campaigns), calling for a reflexive and flexible engagement with the state that does not simply work to reverse those discourses (by, most notably, essentializing homosexuality), but seeks, instead, to denaturalize heteronormativity. Using the analogy of religious disestablishmentarianism, Duggan seeks to expose (and then trouble) the heteronormative state rather than assume its fixity. Both Duggan and Cooper (and, as discussed below, Michael Brown) call for some form of anti-essentialist perspective on the state, and a flexible response (or set of responses) to its power – that it can be used as well as resisted, and that resistance must take on many forms.

Duggan differs from Cooper in her response to transgression, however, noting that while queer politics is 'claiming public and cultural space in imaginative new ways... the politics of the state are generally being left to lesbian and gay civil rights strategies' (Duggan, 1995, p. 186). In the face of new strains of homophobia – especially what might be termed the 'conservative constructionism' of 'contagious' homosexuality – the retreat into strategic essentialism (increasingly the bedrock of rights-based arguments) is, for

Duggan, an untenable tactic. Turning the tables, and deconstruct-
ing heterosexuality by focusing on the state's role in 'promoting
heterosexuality' instead, offers up a better way to approach the
state, Duggan argues, echoing Cooper's point that 'proactive heterosexual strategies are naturalized into invisibility' in state discourse
(Cooper, 1995, p. 69). As part of this deconstructive strategy,
Duggan proposes the use of analogies of neither 'class' (used in
essentialist calls for 'equal protection') nor 'lifestyle' (as seen in
Evans' 'consumer homosexuality'), but rather of religious dissent
– which, she argues, are equally embedded and legible in popular
discourses – to argue for an end to state discrimination:

> If sexual desire is compared to religion, we can see it as not natural,
> fixed, or ahistorical, yet not trivial or shallow, as the term 'lifestyle
> choice' implies. Religion is understood not as biological or fixed; for
> instance, people can and do convert. But it is also understood as a
> deep commitment. That commitment is seen as highly resistant to
> coerced conversion, and deserving of expression and political pro-
> tection.   (Duggan, 1995, p. 190)

While the actions of the religious right might make the use of
religious analogy seem unpalatable – and while Duggan elides the
inherent bigotry within some religions (who view those of other
faiths as misled) – the rhetorical power of such an assertion certainly offers a viable alternative model of agitation to those currently mobilized. While Cooper also echoes Duggan's call to queer
the state, albeit in the more speculative form of a question – 'What
might a queer or lesbian state look like?' (Cooper, 1995, p. 73) – the
two part company over the value of strategies, such as Duggan's
sexual disestablishmentarianism, that work primarily at the level of
the symbolic: 'the emphasis placed by many activists on symbolic
change sometimes deflects attention from whether new possibilities
are actually being realized, or whether the only change is at the
level of prefigurative signifiers, the discursive 'as ifs' of a brave new
world' (Cooper, 1995, p. 73).

   Such an easy separation between the 'symbolic' and the 'real'
seems at odds with Cooper's pluralist strategies (though not, perhaps, with her take on transgression), while her call for 'equal
empowerment' chimes with Duggan's attempt to find new ways

of even talking about sexual citizenship. Nevertheless, Cooper's attempts to reshape the state – and to reshape our ways of thinking the state – are of considerable assistance in reconceptualizing modes of political empowerment and modes of citizenship, including dissident citizenship. As we shall see in our discussion of the sexual and the social in chapter 4, however, this tension between symbolic and real endures within debates on sexual politics and theory in a problematic way.

In looking around for lessons in how to activate new models of citizenship, Duggan points to work in the arts that has brought 'theory' into public discourse, and to similar cross-overs in AIDS work: 'activists working on the issues surrounding the AIDS crisis managed to transport the work of theory into the arena of politics and public policy with astonishing speed and commitment' (1995, p. 186). Likewise, Cooper's account of 'engagement with the state' looks at the complex relationships – not straightforwardly antagonistic – formed between the (local and national) state and AIDS organizations.

AIDS citizenship

A more sustained analysis of 'AIDS citizenship' is contained within Michael Brown's *RePlacing Citizenship* (1997). Brown's mission is to locate (in both senses of the word) Chantal Mouffe's radical democratic citizen in the spaces of AIDS work in Vancouver, and also to critique Mouffe's imagining of citizenship by thinking *geographically* about how citizenship is both empowered and constrained in space. Brown's way into these debates and critiques is through an ethnography of spaces of AIDS citizenship in one city – Vancouver. This leads him into a consideration of the complex interplay between these 'spaces' – often abstracted in political theory as the state, civil society and the private sphere – through the particular forms of AIDS citizenship mobilized in each and, more importantly, in the interstices between them, which Brown labels 'hybrid spaces'. Drawing on poststructuralist decentrings of the subject, Brown asks for a similar theoretical decentring of these spaces, pointing to the political inefficacy of maintaining fixed (essentialized) notions of and relationships to them (most notably in his discussion of ACT UP Vancouver's 'failure', explained by Brown by their fixed idea of the state and their singular, oppositional stance towards it from within civil society). So, although Brown divides his study up along the axis of spatialized politics, he is explicitly concerned with muddying these distinctions.

Brown's study also raises the problematic negotiation between incorporation and opposition, arguing that '[b]ureaucratization and clientization remain constant threats to the critical potential of radical democratic citizenship', since the assumed identities of citizen, client and bureaucrat are similarly fixed: 'Their identities rest on familiar, well-defined characterizations. In the citizens that we imagine, the voters, grassroots volunteers, and clients are recipients of urban services, while the bureaucrats are the paid employees, professionals, and experts inside of, and embodying, the state' (p. 85). Such a separation of roles and identities is, for Brown, both inaccurate and unhelpful. Nevertheless, as Cooper also discusses, the dread of clientization and bureaucratization – of, that is, state incorporation – impacts negatively on the paths taken by individual and collective engagements with welfare activism. For Brown, the notion of the 'shadow state' – voluntary organizations linked to the state via funding and contracting – complicates this relationship.

Perhaps the most useful sections of *RePlacing Citizenship* are chapters 5 and 6, focusing on the interplay of public (state and civil society) and private (home and family) spaces of AIDS citizenship. In the latter, Brown considers the AIDS Quilt as a public enunciation (or memorialization) of grief and rage – a kind of subaltern counterpublic – which is simultaneously a site for both consciousness-raising (and fund-raising) and for the public affirmation of kinship and collectivity: a 'time-space event of citizenship in civil society' (p. 183) that is many-layered, polysemic, *both* personal *and* public. In this way, he argues, the Quilt creates a hybrid space between family and civil society – or, we might say, between intimacy and citizenship.

The second public/private hybrid space Brown explores is embodied in the buddy programme – in the space between the home and the (shadow) state. Buddying, Brown argues, is uniquely placed to further this interplay of intimacy and citizenship, emphasizing new forms of kinship made in and through the buddying relationship. Crucially – and very problematically, as we shall see – this leads Brown to call for a broadening of our ideas about the place(s) of citizenship to include 'locations like the home, the bedside, and even the coffee shop. We must therefore see it in relationships that are full of love and tenderness and especially support as much as those that take the form of social work and personal advocacy' (p. 29).

It is immensely revealing that Brown lists the bedside *but not the bed*, the coffee shop *but not the sex shop*, as 'new' spaces of sexual citizenship (see also Binnie, 1998; Dangerous Bedfellows, 1996). There are echoes here of the conservative gay agenda, as represented in the USA by writers such as Bruce Bawer and Andrew Sullivan. In an essay on Sullivan, Phillip Harper quotes from an 'AIDS-patient advocate' interviewed in Sullivan's 1996 *New York Times* article on the 'end of AIDS'. The interviewee is trying to think about reorienting his life in the wake of this end: 'It's a big world and at some point you have to find a way to slip back into it and try to be a happy citizen. What I want is a boyfriend I love, a job that doesn't make me crazy and good friends' (Sullivan, 1996, p. 58, quoted in Harper, 1997, p. 12). Upon quoting this, Harper comments: 'Exactly how these latter items constitute "citizenship", happy or otherwise ... – and, indeed, why a pleasant existence should be construed specifically in terms of citizenship in the first place – is not at all clear to me' (p. 12). It is equally unclear, of course, why these kinds of formulation emphasize love and friendship but not sex – and it is especially ironic to see Brown delimit AIDS citizenship to these sites 'full of love and tenderness' when one reads Cindy Patton's Foreword to *RePlacing Citizenship*, for she finds radical citizenship on the streets and in cruising grounds. Where is the place for *erotic citizenship* in Brown's (or, for that matter, Sullivan's) formulation? This ambivalent mapping of the spaces of citizenship is a recurrent theme of our subsequent discussions.

Before that, though, we want to stay with Brown's 'new' spaces of citizenship a moment longer, as his cosy coffee shop and bedside intimacy is partly echoed in Ken Plummer's call, in *Telling Sexual Stories* (1995), for a rethinking of citizenship through notions of the intimate. Echoing Giddens' and Weeks' proposed shift to 'life politics', Plummer finds in modes of 'sexual storytelling' the narratives for a new order of citizenship based around the family, the emotions, notions of readership and representation, the body, gender, identity and the erotic. Jeffrey Weeks' discussion of the 'moment of citizenship' likewise attempts to redraw maps of sexual citizenship (which we shall give attention to throughout *The Sexual Citizen*). All of these commentators stress new core values for this kind of citizenship – Weeks (1995, p. 172) calls it a 'love ethic' combining care, responsibility, respect and knowledge (values also found in Steven Seidman's (1992) 'pragmatic sexual ethic' as well as in Giddens' (1992) guide to the 'transformation of intimacy'). The forms such a love ethic takes in these theorizations – and the boundaries drawn, especially in relation to sexual practice – require us to interrogate critically the concept of love itself. This task is taken up in chapter 8.

Echoing Plummer's call to read 'representational stories' as part of intimate citizenship is Diane Richardson's (1998) fusing of Jan Pakulski's (1997) writing on 'cultural citizenship' with questions of sexual identity. Pakulski adds a set of 'representational' or 'cultural' rights to those usually associated with citizenship: the right to symbolic presence and visibility, the right to endignifying representation, and the right to define modes of identity and lifestyle – what might be read together as 'the right to be "different" ' (p. 83). In the light of pressures for assimilation among gay conservatives, and the moral rhetorics of sexual privacy, these additional rights claims mark an important reorientation of sexual citizenship, which we shall be turning to throughout this book.

Queering citizenship

Lisa Duggan's call to 'queer the state' might find its equal in a call to queer the citizen. But what would such a queering entail? For us, part of the answer must be to bring in the erotic and embodied dimensions excluded in many discussions of citizenship – to look at the street and cruising grounds, as Cindy Patton suggests, and to find new spaces of dissident sexual citizenship that do not seek to deny the presence of such erotic topographies. Against Brown's tale of ACT UP Vancouver's 'failure', then, we must set other tales of radical democratic citizenship enacted by queer bodies in public space – such as those found in Ty Geltmaker's (1997) account of AIDS and queer activism in Los Angeles. Describing the body (or, rather, *his* body) as 'politically trespassed public space' (p. 237), Geltmaker describes the tense negotiations around health care and sexual politics in 'Fortress LA' – the city, like the body, as a battle-ground. Similarly, Stanley Aronowitz's (1995) discussion of ACT UP New York sketches resistance to processes of bureaucratization and clientization, finding a distinct conception of citizenship articu-lated in its 'ultra-democratic', anti-hierarchical style of organization – a 'movement' that resists becoming an 'organization', resists being sucked into the shadow state, and that pulls together a set of radical, transgressive strategies of refusal (refusal to act 'appro-priately', refusal to follow familiar campaigning routes, refusal to buy into liberal-statist grammars of rights and welfare) to build a subaltern counterpublic. By trying to remain outside of the logic of the liberal state, ACT UP's actions reshape the terrain of citizenship and change the very ways of talking about it. As Thomas Yingling (1991, p. 299) writes, the imperative of AIDS activism becomes 'to shift the language game, to speak, demonstrate, and demand in ways that are seen as inappropriate to the game when the game erases them or excludes them from its continual reformulation'.

A more recent reappraisal of ACT UP New York's activism, how-ever, paints a rather different picture; one that doesn't refuse the rules of the game. Peter Cohen's (1997) discussion of American middle-class white gay male culture suggests, *contra* Aronowitz, that ACT UP New York – precisely because of its membership's 'class style' (as affluent gay consumers working largely 'within the system') – progressively blunted its radicalism, pushing the agenda towards a more moderate, liberal-statist reform politics, stressing that a modest intervention aimed at selectively reshaping existing institutions could adequately address the needs of people with HIV. Cohen locates this shift almost entirely in terms of the class privi-leges (including freedom to consume) that positioned key members of ACT UP New York in a collaborative rather than confrontational relationship to the state. Central to Cohen is the class-based assumption of *entitlement* – that the system *should* be helping (because that is what these men had come to expect). True, ACT UP was responsible for some of the most dazzlingly visible forms of public protest around HIV and AIDS, but Cohen argues that this was increasingly sidelined by strategies for working with and within existing institutions – especially as ACT UP New York's focus became on finding a cure, through liaison with drug com-panies and the FDA. Further, the secure funding base of ACT UP, the amounts of media savvy (thus ensuring high-profile coverage for their more spectacular actions) and the organizational skills of members combined to create a form of what Cohen calls 'bourgeois militancy' (p. 105), which muted its more radical, transgressive approach (this became a 'last resort' if more accommodationist strategies failed to yield results).

It is important, however, to note that Cohen, like Brown and Geltmaker, is at pains to point out that his account of ACT UP is specifically located in space and time – and, as Aronowitz makes clear, part of ACT UP's radicalism comes from its loose and local organizational stance, so the assessments made here have to be set in their particular context, and not inferred as representing the sum of ACT UP's approach and methods. The politics of rage and the politics of the body enacted by queer and AIDS activists, in fact, might take us some way towards thinking queer citizenship (once we have noted the comments made above) – and, perhaps, of imagining a queer counterpublic (a notion we return to repeatedly in subsequent chapters). Cohen makes a further point about the contradictory impacts of the AIDS crisis on middle-class American gay men in relation to activism: that such 'bourgeois' privacy had actually been central to maintaining their class privileges – permitting them to 'pass' in public situations – but that the necessity of mobilizing around AIDS forced forms of collective visibility that radically reconstituted their social identities and positions: 'AIDS dislodged certain gay men from their tenuous position within the dominant classes by transforming unmarked individuals into members of a stigmatized group' (p. 87). While Cohen suggests this was an uncomfortable transformation, its broader impacts have been to reconfigure relationships to privacy precisely by reinvesting it with notions of repression, secrecy and shame.

Such a resistance of privacy has in fact become central not just to AIDS activism but also to other political agitations around sexual citizenship – around censorship, around sex education, around prostitution and around public sex. The Dangerous Bedfellows collective's *Policing Public Sex* (1996) gives us a picture of this vital strand of dissident sexual-citizenship theorizing and activism. Beginning with a question from Lisa Duggan (p. ix) – 'What's a queer activist to do?' – the collection argues against not only homophobic policing and prevention by state agencies, but (equally crucially) the 'moralizing new gay politics' (p. xi) that colludes in policing erotic spaces. These erotic spaces, David Serlin argues, are perhaps the central sites for a queer counterpublic – for reformulating a liberatory sexual politics away from the model of the 'good gay citizen'. As he concludes, 'commercial establishments for public sex play an important role not merely in affirming the right to consume porn or patronize sex clubs, but in supporting the construction of an alternative economy that encourages the desire for sexual *and* political liberation (1996, p. 52, emphasis in original). By redrafting the war on 'sexual deviance' through the bourgeois master-trope of property (through zoning regulations, planning prohibitions and so on), the debate gets made over as a contest over territory, its uses and its value: *sexual geography rewritten as economic geography* (Binnie, 1998). This kind of situation urges us to consider the economic and the social as crucial sites (and spaces) for the contestations of sexual citizenship – a theme taken up in subsequent chapters.

The effect of this reorientation, of course – indeed, as many contributors to *Policing Public Sex* make clear, the effect of the many ways in which intimacy is reinscribed morally through logics inspired, in large part, by the AIDS crisis – is to *reprivatize* sexual citizenship. Lauren Berlant suggests that privatizing citizenship itself has been as key aim of new right politics; in *The Queen of America Goes to Washington City* (1997) she details the moves that have resulted in what she calls a '[d]ownsizing [of] citizenship to a mode of voluntarism and privacy' (p. 5). Berlant also foregrounds the AIDS crisis as a crucial turn away from the (heterosexually inscribed) 'sexual revolution':

> The transformation in national sexual culture from thinking about sexuality in terms of lives already in progress to imagining sexuality in the shadow of deaths to be avoided registers a shift in the contours of national personhood that is widely experienced, but little narrated. This is a revolution that has forced a generation of sexual subjects to become conscious of a much larger variety of life practices, and to see that these constitute a field of choices and identifications ordinary people make. (p. 16)

Echoing the comments made by Cooper, Berlant notes the ambiguous double effect of the AIDS crisis – bringing an increased public consciousness of queer culture while also mobilizing new forms of homophobia; in addition, by calling into question the modal form of the citizen, there has been a reinvestment in the family as the locus of American life; as Linda Singer (1993, p. 68) has written, the appropriation of safer sex messages into this discourse has led to the 'remaking [of] the nuclear family as a prophylactic social device'.

The impact of this rewrite of the AIDS crisis has, further, been to spawn a 'virulent form of revitalized national heterosexuality' that is 'complexly white and middle class', and which deploys 'cruel and mundane strategies both to promote shame for non-normative populations and to deny them state, federal, and juridical supports because they are deemed morally incompetent to their own citizenship' (Berlant, 1997, p. 19). This moral incompetence is part of a process of infantalization that Berlant locates in Reaganite rhetoric and policy; exactly the same kind of infantalization can be seen at work in the authoritarian populism of both new right and centre-left governments in the UK.

Berlant also shares an interest with the Dangerous Bedfellows collective in public sex (see also Berlant and Warner, 1998), high-lighting the transgressive threat posed by what she calls 'sex acts on the live margin', by which she means 'sex acts that threaten because they do not aspire to the privacy protection of national culture, nor the narrative containment of sex into one of the conventional romantic forms of modern consumer heterosexuality' (Berlant, 1997, p. 62). Against the normative construction of the sexual citizen, where the body is decontextualized and national culture is 'patriarchalized and parentalized', sex radicals have sought to 'countercorporealize' (p. 80), to resist being drawn into the zone of privacy. This is explored in a later chapter of *The Queen of America* through the activities of Queer Nation (and, as we have seen already, in the case of ACT UP). The troubling notion of privacy, central to certain forms of sex-political agitation, must therefore, for Berlant, be jettisoned, however potentially dangerous it may seem, if a new theory of sexual citizenship is to be formulated and enacted.

The notion of 'consumer heterosexuality' that Berlant uses in her talk of 'live sex acts' bounces us down to her later discussion of 'free-market patriotism'. Davina Cooper's reading of the UK's Citizen's Charter (1993) traces a similar reorientation of modalities of citizenship through the logic of the market: renaming welfare recipients as 'customers' or 'clients', thereby depoliticizing and individuating them by framing them within a sovereign-consumerist discourse with no room for collective protest – as Cooper points out, it is 'a citizen's charter rather than citizens' charter' (p. 160). We might read this against the grain of Evans' (1993) 'virilisation' of commercialized gay male sexuality, then, to rethink the relationships between sexual citizenship and the market in terms of the economic impacts of such customerization.

This critical overview of assorted formulations of sexual citizenship has brought us closer to the moment of definition. However, we want to discuss here two further recent discussions of sexual citizenship, framed in particular ways, that offer us alternative versions to work with; out of our critical reading of these, we shall arrive at our own understanding of the question of who the sexual citizen is.

How to be a sexual citizen

Diane Richardson (1998) has attempted to survey and summarize existing insights into sexual citizenship, and we would like to sketch her argument here, as well as that made by Jeffrey Weeks (1999). Both writers seek to explore how the notion of sexual citizenship is currently mobilized. Richardson's focus shadows that of feminist critiques of citizenship discourse, by exposing the heterosexualizing of citizenship as an extension of exposing its gendering: 'My starting point is the argument that claims to citizenship status, at least in the West, are closely associated with the institutionalisation of heterosexual as well as male privilege' (1998, p. 88). Following the delineation of the domains of citizenship derived from the work of T. H. Marshall – civil, political and social – she charts inequalities faced by two groups of sexual citizens, lesbians and gay men: lack of full and equal rights, lack of full political participation and representation, lack of access of welfare entitlements. While she acknowledges that lesbians and gay men are afforded certain rights – usually won as a result of their designation as a 'minority group' – she argues that there is a very high price to pay: sexual citizenship is heavily circumscribed and simultaneously privatized, its limits set

by the coupling of tolerance with assimilation: '[l]esbians and gay
men are granted the right to be tolerated as long as they stay within
the boundaries of that tolerance, whose borders are maintained
through a heterosexist public/private divide' – this means that
lesbians and gay men can be citizens only if they can be 'good'
citizens (p. 90). This cost, in terms of performing 'good' sexual
citizenship, is identified by Carl Stychin (1998, p. 200) as one of
the prime dangers in using citizenship as a model for advancing
lesbian and gay rights claims: 'in attempting to achieve legal vic-
tories, lesbians and gays seeking rights may embrace an ideal of
"respectability", a construction that then perpetuates a division
between "good gays" and (disreputable) "bad queers".... The latter
are then excluded from the discourse of citizenship'.

In addition, Richardson notes that limiting lesbians' and gay
men's spaces of citizenship to the private has a contradictory logic
to it, in that the private sphere is constructed in a heterosexualized
frame, as the space of the family. This helps explain the enduring
deployment of reformulations of 'family' in current sexual rights
claims – in the notion of 'families we choose' and in arguments for
lesbian and gay marriage and parenting: the model of the private
into which sexual citizens are projected is one in which only certain
articulations are conceivable, as we have already noted and will
witness again and again throughout *The Sexual Citizen*. In terms
of social citizenship, Richardson defines this in the context of
the nation-state, in terms of social membership or belonging. As
the growing literature on the relationship between sexuality and the
nation shows, despite the imperatives of globalization and trans-
nationalism, citizenship continues to be anchored in the nation,
and the nation remains heterosexualized. The arguments over
military exclusion of sexual dissidents in the USA and UK can be
seen as emblematic of the tensions between sexual and national
identity, as we shall see.

Finally, Richardson signals two domains of citizenship not considered by Marshall, but which have come to be seen as central to
contemporary citizenship discourses: cultural citizenship and citizenship as consumerism. The first includes struggles over representation and 'symbolic rights', while the second centres on the
economic and commercial power of groups to 'buy' themselves
rights and recognition, as we have already seen. The sum of

Richardson's argument, then, is that citizenship is inevitably a heterosexualized concept, such that rights claims based on citizenship status mobilized by lesbians and gay men must be moulded to fit this pre-existing heterosexual frame: citizenship is always already sexualized, we are all always already sexual citizens, but we are differently marked in terms of our sexual citizenship status, in terms of how our sexual identity fits (or doesn't fit) with the prescribed, naturalized heterosexual presumptive of the notion of citizenship itself.

Jeffrey Weeks' (1999) essay 'The sexual citizen' approaches the subject from a very different angle. Weeks' interest is in the broader social transformations that have created the preconditions for the figure of the sexual citizen to emerge on the landscape of citizenship:

> The sexual citizen, I want to argue, could be male or female, young or old, black or white, rich or poor, straight or gay: could be anyone, in fact, but for one key characteristic. The sexual citizen exists – or, perhaps better, wants to come into being – because of the new primacy given to sexual subjectivity in the contemporary world. . . . [T]his new personage is a harbinger of a new politics of intimacy and everyday life. (p. 35)

Set against this backdrop of transformations in identity, intimacy and relationships, this 'new personage', the sexual citizen, is heroized as shifting the very grounds of politics through a version of Giddens' (1991) 'reflexive project of the self':

> The idea of sexual or intimate citizenship is simply an index of the political space that needs to be developed rather than a conclusive answer to it. But in this new world of infinite possibility, but also ever-present uncertainty, we need pioneers, voyagers, experimenters with the self and with relationships. The would-be sexual citizen, I suggest, represents that spirit of searching and of adventure. (Weeks, 1999, p. 48)

In this sense the sexual citizen, as Weeks conceives him or her, is a marker of transformations in the sphere of personal life, and particularly in its politicization, that have taken place in the West since the 1960s. Weeks sketches the transformations that have created the possibility of the sexual citizen as threefold: (1) the democratization of relationships (new ways of living together); (2) new subjectivities (new forms of identity and new notions of the self); and (3) new stories (new ways of narrativizing (1) and (2) in, for example, counterdiscourses). He ends with a list of issues 'likely to be central to post millennial politics':

> achieving a new settlement between men and women;
> elaborating new ways of fulfilling the needs for autonomy and mutual involvement that the family can no longer (if it ever could) fulfil;
> finding ways of dealing with the denaturalization of the sexual: the end of the heterosexual/homosexual binary divide, the new reproductive technologies, the queering of identities;
> balancing the claims of different communities with constructing new common purposes, recognizing the benefits of individual choice while affirming the importance of collective endeavours;
> learning to live with diversity at the same time as building our common humanity. (p. 49)

While Weeks is keen to stress that this is neither an agenda nor a map, his utopian projection of twenty-first-century politics clearly (while also rather vaguely) lists new domains of sexual citizenship without offering concrete proposals for the materialization of his wishes. It's almost as if merely living as a sexual citizen will inevitably bring about these further transformations. In fact, in many ways, that kind of logic steers some of the current ways in which the rights claims of sexual citizens are argued: that lesbian and gay marriage, for example, could serve to undermine, even destroy, the whole institution of marriage and all its attendant privileges, from within (as we shall see in chapter 3).

As we have already noted, central to Weeks' argument is the distinction between strategies for acceptance ('the moment of citizenship') and strategies of subversion ('the moment of transgression'). In an earlier essay, Weeks suggests that the two are necessary elements of an overall political project: '[b]oth moments are essential to the opening-up of space for the social recognition of diverse ways of life, even if the carnival of difference and the sober suits of integration do not always mix' (1995, p. 118). The logic of Weeks' argument – of the need for both transgression and incorporation – is further sketched out in a 'conversation' with Sue Golding:

What I suggest is that in any radical political movement there's always the moment of transgression when you try to pull the pillars down, when you try to challenge the *status quo*. . . . But linked to that is the moment of citizenship, which is the moment of making claims on society, a claim for inclusion. Making that claim for inclusion may seem assimilationist, but actually making demands on a culture which denies you is extremely radical: it identifies the frontiers of the conventional, it demarcates the lines of struggle. So, you can see transgression and citizenship as simply different faces of the same moment of challenge. One is separating, the other is calling for belonging. But you can only do one with the other. (Weeks, 1997, p. 323)

From here, Weeks offers a somewhat strange justification for the necessary twinning of transgression and inclusion:

that moment of transgression is needed by those who argue for citizenship, for belonging, so you can say, 'look, if you don't let us in, there are all these weirdos out there, including us, who will go on being disruptive. And the weirdos out there who are also us can also say we're different, but we also want this difference to be recognized and this difference can only be recognized in the transformation of citizenship'. (p. 323)

Transgression here seems to operate as some kind of threat or irritation – a *weirdness* that is disruptive and annoying, but that will dissipate upon the transformation of citizenship. The 'carnival of difference', then, is a lever for inclusion; transgression has its political place in Weeks' argument, to be sure, but only *strategically*. Elizabeth Wilson (1993, p. 116) makes a similar point about transgression: 'it can only ever be a tactic, never a total politics'; it is, she says, 'a word of weakness' (p. 113), always reactive, never productive. And while both Weeks and Wilson argue for a third way of politics, which in some ways combines the moment of transgression and the moment of citizenship, their tone suggests that transgression is merely to be tolerated – it's a noisy, unruly toddler that'll soon grow up; a phase to be gone through. Their positions seem seriously to undervalue transgression, subversion and resistance as cornerstones of sexual politics, and both seem to dismiss transgression's role without considering its rhetorical power.

Toby Miller engages with the question of transgression at length in *The Well-Tempered Self* (1993), through a discussion of 'incivility' embodied in the actions of two members of the Sisters of Perpetual Indulgence (an order of gay male nuns) during a visit to Sydney University by Pope John Paul II in 1986. Describing their activities as a 'carnival-like anti-program' (p. 206), Miller stresses the politics of location and visibility as central to the Sisters' incivility – central to their enactment of 'the resistive gay as a misbehaving public cultural subject' (p. 216). Such a strategic strike throws into question the transgression-versus-incorporation dualism common to theorizations of citizenship, offering a riposte to those theories that would seek to see transgression as a mere sideshow or as an embarrassment. Miller's discussion should, once and for all, make clear that such actions are important, indeed necessary, components of the struggle for dissident sexual citizenship; while commentators like Weeks quite casually stereotype the 'carnival of difference' and the 'sober suits of integration' (what about the sober suits of transgression? what about the meeting of the two approaches, often in the same person, petitioning one day and attending a die-in the next?), Miller makes it clear that we need to explore more fully the logics of both forms of activism in the context of their situatedness in particular discourses of citizenship – to see queer counterpublics as spaces of sexual citizenship.

While both Richardson and Weeks argue that we are all sexual citizens – or at least, in Weeks' discussion, *potential* sexual citizens – there are fundamental differences in their formulations. Richardson's focus is more on critique – on exposing citizenship as heterosexualized, and on exploring rights claims in that context. As such, her argument helps us to establish the ground on which to explore particular articulations of sexual citizenship; her essay must make us ask a question that we shall return to throughout this book: given the heterosexualization of citizenship, how can rights claims based on citizenship status from sexual minorities be made to work other than by replicating heterosexualized articulations of the 'good citizen'? Will the figure of the 'good gay citizen' merely prop up this heterosexualization, or could the 'good gay citizen' work to undermine the heterosexual presumption of citizenship status?

Weeks' argument, by contrast, focuses on the self-conscious articulation of sexual citizenship as a mode of life politics in late modernity. In line with Giddens' thesis in *The Transformation of Intimacy* (1992), Weeks suggests that remaking the terms and conditions of intimate interpersonal relations can be a revolutionary act in itself. As we shall see in chapter 8, the transformation of intimacy can be read as opening up new ways of living and loving that *might* break up the heterosexualized model of citizenship delineated by Richardson. Essentially, Weeks is suggesting that the reshaping of personal life has brought sexual politics centrestage, thereby shifting the meaning of citizenship to take greater account of the sexual. At that level we have to agree with him: sexuality has become more prominent in mainstream politics, and not just oppositionally; notions of sexual rights and sexual justice are beginning to receive greater attention in law and politics. What this means for Weeks is an extension of the bounds of citizenship itself.

Such an extension is proposed by Ken Plummer's (1995) discussion of 'intimate citizenship' – a notion that Weeks draws on. Aside from the familiar social, political and civic components of citizenship, then, Plummer proposes *intimate citizenship* as an additional framework for addressing sexual politics. The first aspect of intimacy he discusses is, in fact, concerned with the family – with the ways in which 'stories of living together' in diverse and multiple ways can be used to rethink the connections between notions of community and notions of citizenship – offering a radical counternarrative ('pretended families', to use Section 28's derisive terminology) to the foreclosing definitions of 'family' clustering in political discourses (see also Nardi, 1992; Weston, 1998). Added to family are emotions, representations, the body, gender, erotics and identities – explored through Plummer's master-trope of storytelling. If we take the sum of Plummer's stories to point towards a citizenship of pleasures, of the private, of experiences, then we can see the merit of such an expansion, perhaps particularly in the context of sexual politics, since the components of intimate citizenship that Plummer identifies have previously been excluded from debate on the grounds that they inhabit the private realm – a realm more or less untouched (maybe even untouchable) by citizenship discourses focused on public life (although not immune, it must be remembered, from state interference). It is, however, also problematic, in as much as opening up or offering up the private as a space for a politics of citizenship can render it vulnerable to other, unintended forms of

political interrogation and intervention. A politics of desire, a politics of the erotic, can bring 'private' issues out into the open
through the legitimating lens of 'the public interest' (Bell, 1995a,
1995b). Further, as we have already noted, making the private
sphere the 'proper home' of sexual citizenship forecloses some of
the 'infinite possibilities' that Weeks sees in the future.

Plummer's utopian vision of a full-bodied citizenship also seems
to disregard the potential perils of storying the self as a sexual
citizen. It sidesteps Davina Cooper's critical analysis of the deployment of 'sex talk' in relation to state power. In 'An engaged state:
sexuality, governance, and the potential for change' (1993a),
Cooper explores the tensions in public-versus-private narratives of
sexuality: either sex is written out as inappropriate to 'the public'
(paradoxically generating forms of 'sex talk' to legitimate this 'pri-
vating'), or its privacy is seen as in need of protection from an
encroaching public scrutiny. In relation to intimacy, Judith Squires
(1994) points to some theorists' stress on a necessary relationship
between the intimate and the private, arguing the need for 'a
defence of privacy and individuality', and that 'such a defence is
just as important as the work being done to revive our sense of
community and citizenship' (p. 398). The perspective adopted here
by both Squires and Cooper suggests a need for caution in the
project Plummer advocates. In fact, in place of privacy, Plummer
talks only of secrecy (and its dangers), arguing the need for 'many
voices' to be heard. The question of who hears those many voices
has to be addressed – and that, in part, is what both Cooper and
Squires turn their attentions to. Cooper's reference to the 'confessional' as a coercive mode of storytelling, for example, suggests that
public exposure need not be politically enabling; there are dangers
in 'going public' (or being made to go public), too. The debate over
gays in the military illustrates these complexities well; we turn our
attention to that debate in chapter 3.

So, yet again, we find ourselves feeling ambivalent about Weeks'
argument that a new politics of everyday life or a greater political
concern with the quality of life inevitably opens up a space for the
sexual citizen to occupy – and that occupying this space might in
and of itself then be more broadly transformative. There remain real
structural limitations to the possibilities for the kinds of experiments
of living that Weeks highlights – some of these are political, some

social, some economic. Those limits may be more elastic than they once were, but this does not necesarily make them any more breachable.

Having sketched the formulations of sexual citizenship offered by Richardson and Weeks, we need finally to arrive at our own working definition. We agree with Richardson on a number of counts: first, that citizenship discourse needs to be recognized as heterosexualized, and that part of the task of the sexual citizen must be to challenge that – so, while we are all sexual citizens, in that citizenship is a particularly contextualized enunciation of identity which must take account of sexual identity – there are different forms of sexual citizenship (a point made by Evans (1993)). Crucially, there is a naturalized, heteronormative modality of sexual citizenship implicit in mainstream political and legal formulations; and set against this, there are myriad forms of what we might label *dissident sexual citizenship*. Different forms of sexual identity mark claims to citizenship status differently – the arguments for transgender rights, for example, have a different agenda from that coming from lesbian and gay politics, although there may be coalitional commonalities and strategic alliances across such dissident sexualities, for example over reproductive rights (Whittle, 1998). In addition to different forms of sexual identity making different forms of sexual citizenship, there are different modalities of citizenship that mark the same sexual categories differently – the gay male citizen, for example, is not a universal figure with the same concerns and politics worldwide (Manalansan, 1995).

To some extent we also want to side with Weeks' notion of the reflexive sexual citizen, if that means that citizenship claims are increasingly being made by individuals and groups who choose to mobilize around their sexual identities – who see sexuality as central to their status as citizens (or non-citizens). While we would want to signal again our ambivalence towards Weeks' overall formulation about citizenship as the 'proper home' of sexual dissidents, given the structural limitations that still mark citizenship in the ways Richardson suggests, we nevertheless do want to give some weight to those 'experiments in living' that he describes the sexual citizen as engaged in. To understand how the sexual citizen has come into being, as Weeks says, we need to look at the broader social and cultural transformations that have occurred. Now, while

Weeks concentrates on new relationships, new identities and new stories of the self, we would rather begin by considering the changing landscape of sexual politics, in order to understand how key shifts here have given shape to the discourses of sexual citizenship that will concern us throughout *The Sexual Citizen*. That is our task in the next chapter.

2

Sexual Politics and Sexual Citizenship

In this chapter we want to explore the context out of which the possibility for sexual citizenship has arisen, by looking at the formations of sexual politics across the 1980s and 1990s. This was a period marked by countless transformations, which we need to talk about here. These transformations include: the controversial appearance, negotiations and disputes around queer theory and queer politics; the centralizing of the AIDS crisis in both mobilizing and allying discourses and in homophobic discourses; continuing debates over notions of 'lesbian and gay community', especially in relation to queer politics and with respect to other sexual dissidents, such as bisexual and transgendered people; varieties of 'sex war' (around pornography and sadomasochism, for example) recasting notions of a politics rooted in desire; the solidifying of social constructionist notions of sexuality through theories of (queer) performativity, versus the contrary re-essentializing of 'gay' identity through biomedical research ('gay brains' and 'gay genes'); the intensified marketization of sexualities, and so on. In the light of these (and other) transformations, then, the field of sexual politics in its broadest sense seemed likewise to embody many of the debates activated by a focus on citizenship, with its crossing of boundaries between the public and the private, between the collective and the individual, between entitlements and duties. What we would like to do here is to expand on this list of changes in the terrain of sexual politics, in order to establish the agendas that have come to inform the articulation of rights claims under the banner of sexual citizenship.

The first and in many ways the most significant shifts in sexual politics are those concerned with the AIDS crisis, and related to that, the emergence of both queer politics and its academic cousin, queer theory. A great deal has already been written about this subject, of course, so we propose here merely to sketch the significant issues that will re-emerge in the subsequent discussions of the sexual citizen. Crucially, the AIDS crisis reshaped the demonization process of sexual minorities (as well as intravenous drug users, 'racial' minorities and a number of other marginalized groups), giving a new political and moral agenda to homophobia, now marked by contagion and 'sexual risk'. The central thrust of this assault focused on promiscuity, leading to the closing-down of sites for public and 'casual' sex, and articulating a mode of 'sexual responsibility' that folds into the notion of the 'good gay citizen'. Out of the AIDS crisis, however, sprang new modes of activism, with groups like ACT UP (AIDS Coalition to Unleash Power) and GMHC (Gay Men's Health Crisis) fighting back against the homophobic imperatives of the state's handling of the AIDS crisis (Crimp and Rolston, 1990; Kayal, 1993). As Michael Brown (1997) argues, the collected modalities of dealing with the AIDS crisis can be read as articulating a new form of sexual citizenship, which we might label AIDS citizenship, as we have already seen.

While there are many dimensions to AIDS interventions, including health promotion initiatives, medical campaigning, forms of collective remembrance and community volunteerism – all of which bear traces of citizenship discourse – we want to draw attention here to the tactics of body-politics and public protest, which made visible the rage against state inaction and homophobia (Aronowitz, 1995). The radicalization of AIDS activism, drawing on the techniques of political protest developed by so-called new social movements, fought back against the state, mobilizing diverse groups around an issue that has reshaped sexual politics profoundly. Part of that reshaping, which we think has to be linked to the tactics and techniques of AIDS activism, is the explosion of queer politics, which arose from the recognition that existing political strategies coming from the lesbian and gay community were impotent in the hyper-homophobic context of new right government in the UK and

USA (spurred on by AIDS and by a new moral agenda of 'family values'). In the face of the new right, a new adversarial politics was called for: it was time for queers to bash back.

Queer politics, then, absorbed some of the theoretical moves made in queer theory, which also emerged at this time – a post-structuralist, postmodern, constructionist view of sexual identity, which the very term 'queer' tried to capture, in an attempt to erase the boundaries that had previously riven sexual communities (Seidman, 1992). While there were (and still are) tensions between academic and activist articulations of queer, the theoretical insights of queer theory nevertheless transformed aspects of sexual politics, creating the opportunity to forge new alliances and set new agendas. And, in reaction to the sex-negativity of state health campaigns in the wake of the AIDS crisis, queer politics came out as proudly pro-sex. Douglas Crimp's (1987) famous call for 'principled promiscuity' as a sex-positive antidote to government puritanism in the age of AIDS marks queer politics as an important site of embodied political resistance, most visibly enacted in public space – space marked as heterosexual, but reclaimed by queer political praxis by media attention-grabbing 'zaps' (Geltmaker, 1997).

Queer politics also threw critical light on the lesbian and gay community and its mode of political activism, arguing that it had settled into an assimilationist agenda, with entryism into mainstream (mainly local) politics and an acceptance of the 'good gay citizen' model. The tension between queer politics and lesbian and gay politics is neatly summed up in a poster advertising the US gay magazine *The Advocate*, from the early 1990s: on the right of the poster, a moustached, thirty-something man says 'I hate it when you use the word "queer"! Your immature tactics are undermining 20 years of gay rights.' On his left, a younger, bandanna-wearing man says 'We're queer! You rich white sell out! Don't you know people are dying and getting bashed!' (see Kader and Piontek, 1992).

Particularly controversial in the collision of these two political agendas has been the 'selling out' strategy of assimilationism, especially where it has sided with state attempts to regulate sexual freedoms (Dangerous Bedfellows, 1996). The collusion of gay rights advocates in campaigns to close down sites for public sex, for example, and the rise of the once oxymoronic 'gay conservative', enraged activists working to turn around the sex negativity of state imperatives. Anti-pornography campaigning, another battleground in the 'sex wars', and debates over sexual practices such as sadomasochism, similarly polarized sexual dissidents, focusing on the question of the 'politics of pleasure' (Duggan and Hunter, 1995). Pervasive sex-negativity, framed as responsibility (the inevitable trade-off to attain rights), met head-on the perverse parade of pleasure-politics that refused the narrowly defined moral code of the 'good gay citizen', finding new ways to articulate responsibility and an ethic of care without having to deny sexual pleasure – indeed, in many cases, by redefining the notion of sexual pleasure itself (Singer, 1993).

Jeffrey Weeks' discussions of the 'moment of transgression' and the 'moment of citizenship', cited earlier, would no doubt slot the public rage and pleasure-politics of queer into the former category, arguing that it's just a phase to be passed through *en route* to a more mature sexual politics in the citizenship model. This seems seriously to undervalue the continued necessity of modes of activism that refuse assimilationist agendas; while we have subtitled our book 'Queer Politics and Beyond' in recognition, perhaps, that the 'moment of queer' has to a large extent passed, we don't mean to diminish the crucial significance of that moment, or to deny its legacy in offering a critique of the consolidation of the 'moment of citizenship' as the mode of sexual politics at the turn of the century. As we have stated already, the 'good gay' and the 'bad queer' are particular ways of marking sexual citizenship status – Weeks seems to suggest, like *The Advocate*'s voice of the gay community, that in the end we'll all grow up to be good sexual citizens, and that the bad (queer) sexual citizen is in fact always a *non-citizen*. The question of who can and cannot be granted the status of sexual citizen is, of course, one whose answer constantly shifts – and we must, therefore, remember the broader political contexts in which the debates of sexual citizenship take place. Crucially, for us, we need to be mindful of the shift in the UK and USA from new right to centre-left governance. How has this shifted the terrain of the debate?

Politics and sexual politics: from new right to centre-left

Writing a decade ago, the question posed by Diana Fuss (1989, p. 112) could encapsulate the position of sexual citizenship in Reagan-

era USA in a straightforwardly oppositional way: 'What does it mean
to be a citizen in a state which programmatically denies citizenship
on the basis of sexual preference?' Within the context of conservative
politics, sexual citizenship is *all about* programmatic denial: in an age
of new right discourses, the battleground is clearly mapped, and
everyone knows which side they're on – the oppositional stance of
queer politics is relatively unambivalent when faced by the Reagen–
Bush and Thatcher–Major administrations. But in a centre-left context, everything is potentially redrawn (even if, in practice, very little
changes that radically, as we shall see); a new terrain suggests new
tactics of engagement. Such rewritings of the political context of
sexual citizenship, however, still remain inevitably tied up with the
questions of membership and inclusion. For while there are citizens –
and while the chances of being counted as a citizen *might* expand in
certain directions – there will always be non-citizens, and there will
also always be those who live precariously on the margins of inclusion and exclusion.

The danger of joining the assimilationist agenda is precisely
that those boundaries of inclusion can be expanded and contracted
at political whim. In order to explore this tension, we'd like to
look at the changing shape of politics in the UK in the wake of so-
called New Labour. Focusing on Tony Blair's uneasy relationship
with sexual citizens should help us to see some of the warning signs
of assimilationism – while New Labour is attempting to distance
itself from its new right predecessor, it seems keen to retain some of
the populist agendas the Tories cemented during the Thatcher
and Major administrations. In a telling essay on 'new feminism'
and Blairite New Labour in the UK, Angela McRobbie detects
a redrawing of the notion of 'family' that is increasingly exclusionary:

> The image of social respectability combined with respect for tradi-
> tional family values leaves New Labour with nothing to say about
> current changes in family life. Questioned on these matters on [the
> radio]...Tony Blair couldn't, or wouldn't, say the word gay in
> relation to family life – indeed he could hardly bring himself to say
> the words single parent. All he could do was repeat the fact that
> children were best looked after by both parents living in the tradi-
> tional family unit.   (1997, p. 165)

Struggles for inclusion within existing political definitions (in this case, of 'the family'), then, can be problematically precarious, as agendas shift and the boundaries of incorporation are relocated. What we have to do here is spend a little time exploring the changing shape of British sexual politics in the light of centre-left government.

The victory of Tony Blair's New Labour in the UK's general election of May 1997 has, inevitably, prompted considerable reaction from lesbian and gay activists. In parallel with the mood surrounding Bill Clinton's move to the White House in the USA, there have been alternating expressions of optimistic excitement and more cautious – at times downright pessimistic – assessments of the likely future impact of New Labour on the map of sexual politics in the UK. In the Introduction to *New Frontiers of Space, Bodies and Gender*, for example, Rosa Ainley writes:

> with the Labour Party in Britain newly installed with a large major-
> ity . . . a pervasive euphoria envelops this land, or this writer at least,
> and it remains to be seen how both policy and culture changes will
> be made to the fabric of the environment of the country and the
> ways in which we perceive and make spaces within it.   (1998, p.
> xvii)

The tone of Ainley's comment is symptomatic of the mixed feelings expressed elsewhere: 'pervasive euphoria' blended with a wait-and-see clause; a sense of huge relief at the end of Conservative rule, and a dream of better things to come – tempered by a slight distrust that promises might not be materialized. And, indeed, the weight of the evidence so far justifies that tempering, meetings between government and gay-rights group Stonewall and the second lowering of the age of consent notwithstanding.

In a review of New Labour's promises and practices, Simon Edge similarly sketches out a mixture of positive vibes and policy compromises. Edge soundbites Stonewall's Angela Mason, who makes a revealing statement about the assumed place of lesbians and gay men in Blair's vision: 'We fit in completely with the government's notion of rights and responsibilities . . . They are try-ing to redefine anti-social behaviour, and by removing homosexu-ality from that category and according us full citizenship rights, they could concentrate on pushing the responsibilities of citizenship' (Edge, 1997, p. 23). Earlier in his article, however, Edge has Mason saying 'The problem is, we're not really part of the New Labour script. These issues will get sorted out if we keep the pressure up, but they haven't thought them through yet' (p. 22). So, according to Mason, the creation of the 'good' (that is, not anti-social) homosexual citizen (aware that their responsibilities represent the payback for their rights) *should* be a New Labour priority, if only the Blairite scriptwriters could think things through (of course, what they are thinking through is the relationship between homosexual rights and opinion poll points). The headlining demand of Edge's article – to become 'Proudly, openly, equally gay' – has given way to defeat; the title of Peter Tatchell's assessment of a year of New Labour finds him, instead, 'Battered, bewildered and betrayed' (Tatchell, 1998, p. 17).

We need, therefore, to examine the shifting sands of Blair's stand on homosexuality, and a good place to start is a speech he delivered in the age of consent debate in February 1994. Articulating a kind of centre-left pseudotolerance, he begins by essentializing homosexuality as grounds for anti- (or perhaps, more appropriately, non-) discrimination: 'It is not against the nature of gay people to be gay; it is in fact their nature. It is what they are. It is different, but that is not a ground for discrimination' (Blair, 1996, p. 186). Later in the speech, and despite the projected image of Blair as a politician who regards 'homophobes with the same disdain his predecessors would have reserved for homosexuals' (Lyttle, 1998, p. 5), he opens up a sizeable gap for the presence of homophobia (in an effort to locate himself absolutely centrally, recognizing equally the rights of homosexuals *and* of homophobes): 'Let me be clear that people are entitled to think that homosexuality is wrong, but they are not entitled to use the criminal law to force that view upon others' (p. 188). And, in his concluding crescendo, he makes a strange allusion to the question of the number of lesbians and gay men in the UK (something that has itself been the subject of considerable debate, as researchers bid to downsize Kinsey's sacred 'one-in-ten' ratio), while placing emphasis on the need for 'society' to deal with 'its' homophobia:

A society that has learned, over time, racial and sexual equality can surely come to terms with equality of sexuality. That is the moral case for change. It is our chance to welcome people – I do not care whether there are 50,000, 500,000 or 5 million; it matters not a damn – into full membership of our society, on equal terms. It is our chance to do good, and we should take it. (p. 189)

There are obviously deep ambiguities in all Blair has to say about the age of consent (though, in fact, his speech says little *about* the age of consent itself, and instead gestures more broadly – we might say more vaguely – to questions of 'rights' or 'equality'; see Moran (1996) for a sustained reading of the complex discourses of 'equality in the law' mobilized in that round of age of consent debates). We need to read New Labour's treatment of sexuality issues within the broader contexts of Blair's 'vision of Britain', of course – and, perhaps most crucially, within the context of New Labour's thinking on broader questions of morality and of 'family values'. Angela McRobbie (1997, p. 166) concludes that '[m]aybe Tony Blair is actually saying, without stating it, that sexual culture has gone too far and that we need to constrain desires and forgo their dangerous currents in favour of the pleasures and rewards of everyday family life'. Tony Blair's espousal of communitarianist and Christian-democratic pseudotolerance has as a central plank a strong articulation of the value(s) of 'the family', redlined to exclude increasing numbers of people. While seeking to distance itself from the insidious new right moral rhetoric of family values – as Blair himself put it in an article for the *Sun* newspaper in 1995, '[w]e want fewer politicans spouting about "family values" and more politicians who value families' (Blair, 1996, p. 250) – the centre-left's invoking of what Judith Stacey (1998, p. 3) calls 'neo-family-values' has had profound impacts on policy orientations in the UK, the USA and elsewhere.

It is important, therefore, to mark the complex repositioning of sexual politics within mainstream party politics, and to recognize the endurance of elements of the new right in the centre-left. A significant legacy is the way in which new right discourses around homosexuality manipulated opinion both within and without lesbian and gay culture, producing a distinction between the 'good homosexual' and the 'bad homosexual' (or queer) – a distinction that solidified in the rise of forms of what might be called gay conservatism, and which continues to fracture lesbian and gay politics. We must therefore examine the workings of this distinction and the rise of gay conservative 'good homosexuality'.

The new right legacy

Perhaps the most sustained critical discussion of the new right and its enduring impacts has come from Anna Marie Smith. In her book *New Right Discourse on Race and Sexuality* (1994) and in a number of essays, Smith has interrogated the inner workings of new right (especially Thatcherite) policy and rhetoric, revealing the full complexity of its constructions of good and bad homosexuals, as well as its attempts to articulate and manage a new right hegemony on questions of sexual identity and practice:

> Thatcherite homophobia did not take the form of a one-dimensional exclusion.... Instead of constructing a singular 'us' versus 'them' frontier, they made every effort to represent themselves as 'tolerant' centrists who were mediating between two extremist camps: the vociferous parents' groups, violent queer-bashers, and the whole 'moral' backlash on the one side, and the flaunting, disease-spreading, child-seducing queer and their corrupt socialist allies on the other. (1997, p. 113)

Thatcherite authoritarian populism thus deployed an 'imaginary assimilable "other"' – the 'good homosexual' – which enabled Thatcherites to 'transform their homophobic extremism into a tolerant, moderate, and *inclusionary* discourse' (p. 115; emphasis in original). Cindy Patton (1995) notes the ways in which the new right raided and transformed progressive politics; moreover, this shift works both ways, as evidenced by the articulations of 'neo-family-values' in centre-left discourse (both Clintonite and Blairite), effectively defining the family exclusively through a patriarchal, heterosexualized, nuclear frame (Stacey, 1998).

Crucial for Smith is the interleaving of the construction of the 'good homosexual/bad homosexual' distinction and prominent 'new racism' and anti-multiculturalism discourses. Most notable are those given in the UK the populist slant of opposing the 'Loony Left', as embodied in progressive policies implemented by bodies such as the GLC, which was particularly demonized by Thatcher (see Cooper, 1994). Thatcherite rhetoric thus created a discourse of what Smith (1997, p. 121) names 'pseudotolerant homophobia'; as she says, Thatcherites 'actually differentiate *homosexualities*, and *promote* a homosexuality of a very specific type – that of the "good homosexual" subject' (Smith, 1994, p. 207, emphasis in original). Supporters of Section 28, the most prominent policy manifestation of this position, thus mobilized a constructionist notion of homosexual identity – by arguing that homosexuality was being promoted (as a 'lifestyle') by lesbian and gay groups – leaving the left (and lesbian and gay activists) arguing an essentialized standpoint (note that this apparently lives on, as witnessed in Tony Blair's age of consent speech quoted earlier). For Smith, the left's alignment with essentialism reveals the poverty of the left's thinking on gender and sexuality.

The construction of 'good' and 'bad' homosexualities within Thatcherite discourse must be read alongside the birth of forms of queer activism during the Thatcher years, for the radical visibility of groups like OutRage! (linked inevitably to the 'Loony Left' through the leadership of Peter Tatchell) had to be repositioned as the work of extremists, set against a 'homosexual mainstream': 'The "good homosexual" was therefore represented as the innocent victim of militant queer activism or as the pawn in a socialist plot. . . . [T]he Thatcherites who passed Section 28 into law were the true representatives of the real homosexual – the closeted majority who disowned lesbian and gay activism' (Smith, 1997, p. 124). A central part of this strategy, then, was the construction of a closeted, self-hating and anti-militant homosexuality, and interpellated into that new political space comes the figure of the gay conservative – a figure rising to prominence in both US and UK sexual politics, birthed by the new right and now welcomed into the centre-left's rewriting of pseudotolerant assimilationism.

Gay conservatives and 'good homosexuals'

The canonical – or at least the best-known and most read – texts of gay conservatism come from the USA: Bruce Bawer's *A Place at the Table: the gay individual in American society* (1993), Andrew Sullivan's *Virtually Normal: an argument about homosexuality* (1996), and Marshall Kirk and Hunter Madsen's *After the Ball: how America will conquer its fear and hatred of gays in the '90s* (1989). Each has its own way of articulating the gay conservative agenda, and of opposing the radicalization of homosexuality in queer politics. Kirk and Madsen, for example, describe contemporary queer culture as '*disgustingly* different' and list some of the stereotypes they find so distasteful: 'men ultrawishy and ultraviolet, Frankensteinian thug-women with bolts in their necks, moustachio'd Dolly Parton wanna-bes, leather-men in boots and whips, ombudsmen of pederasty squiring their ombudsboys' (p. 143). They urge instead 'self-policing' of behaviour by homosexuals, offering a help-list of incantations: 'I won't have sex in public places; I won't talk gay sex and gay raunch in public; if I'm a pederast or sadomasochist, I'll keep it under wraps, and out of gay pride marches' (p. 360). As Anna Marie Smith says, for Kirk and Madsen homophobia becomes relegated to a mere 'public relations problem' (Smith, 1997, p. 127) – if homosexuals could learn to present themselves in less disgustingly different ways, homophobia would be eradicated (in fact, virtually everything is translated into a PR issue for them: AIDS and public sex are also tackled in this way in *After the Ball*).

Harper's essay on Sullivan similarly stresses the 'fetish of norm-ativity' in gay conservatism, and it is worth having a closer look at Sullivan's project here. In effect, what Sullivan wishes to do is to *depoliticize* homosexuality – to cast off its aura of radicality and transgression – and to slot it into mainstream American values. This makes gay conservatism a particular (and particularly troub-ling) version of Weeks' moment of citizenship. After reviewing alternative political perspectives on homosexuality, Sullivan con-cludes that politics doesn't hold the answers for 'gay liberation' (though he would never use such a left-tinged term):

> Our battle, after all, is not for political victory but for personal integrity. In the same way that many of us had to leave our families in order to join them again, so now as citizens, we have to embrace politics if only ultimately to be free of it. . . . [P]olitics cannot do the work of life. Even culture cannot do the work of life. Only life can do the work of life. (1996, pp. 187, 168)

The last chapter of *Virtually Normal*, which follows Sullivan's line of argument that heterosexuals and homosexuals must learn from each other, asks and then answers a question: 'What Are Homosexuals For?' This is what he says gays contribute to society: style; irony; childlessness (which means they can work harder, volunteer harder, 'parent' in other ways and displace familial affection on to the broader community); commitment (akin to Giddens' 'pure relationships'); cultural and entrepreneurial regeneration (especially as they are child-free); and lastly rebelliousness:

> It is as if homosexuals have learned something about life that makes them immune to the puritanical and flattening demands of modern politics. It is as if they have learned that life is fickle; that there are parts of it that cannot be understood, let alone solved; that some things lead nowhere and mean nothing; that the ultimate exercise of freedom is not a programmatic journey but a spontaneous one.   (p. 204)

Most incredibly – and this is something we shall return to – Sullivan suggests that the only 'political work' needed to gain lesbian and gay equality is the legalization of gay marriage. This is, in fact, a common strand to all of the gay conservative manifestos (see Pendleton, 1996, for a fuller discussion); Bruce Bawer also keenly advocates gay marriage, in part to end the 'sham marriages' that closeted gay men are forced to enter into in order to maintain normalcy. If only gay men could enter into 'normal society' by marrying each other, he argues, 'one might imagine a gay couple that most heterosexuals would not even recognize as gay' (1993, p. 34) – they would not take part in Queer Nation activities, or live in (or frequent bars and clubs in) a recognizable gay ghetto, or have politics that are 'uncomfortably left-wing' (p. 34). *After the Ball* adds sex-negativity to this argument: 'We're not fighting for the right to suck and fuck . . . we're fighting for the right to love and marry, not merely to blast away with our "hot love-guns"' (Kirk and Madsen, 1989, p. 380). This, then, is the gay conservative's dream: invisibility and total assimilation into mainstream (for which read: white, middle-class, suburban) America:

The world that gay conservatives imagine is a white, suburban, domestic idyll, with gay and straight couples attending dinner parties together, joining the PTA, and swapping recipes over the backyard fence. Left politics of any sort, including feminism, have no place in this universe. Gay conservatives often distance themselves from lesbianism, tainted by its association with feminism, and construct a gay community reminiscent of a gentleman's social club. (Pendleton, 1996, p. 375)

What particularly disturbs Anna Marie Smith about the rise of gay conservatism is its packaging as centrist common sense. More tellingly, she adds that 'centrist and liberal leaderships have not launched an all-out war to win back even the few liberal democratic gains that have been made in the postcolonial, post-civil rights era. They are, instead, all too willing to accommodate the authoritarian populist right' (Smith, 1997, p. 134) – suggesting that the new right legacy lives on in centre-left administrations. Certainly, given the continued demonization of the 'militant (bad) homosexual' and the limited political gestures made thus far (all towards restricted assimilation), there would indeed seem to be plenty of room in the centre-left project for the kinds of ideas and identities promoted by gay conservatives.

There are, of course, many other strands to trace in the solidifying of a good homosexual/bad homosexual distinction. For example, Les Moran (1996) discusses a number of 'uses of homosexuality', focusing on legal discourses that have moved to frame this distinction in particular ways. He uses the case of *Dudgeon v. United Kingdom* (1982) – arguing that the Sexual Offences Act 1967 should be applied in Northern Ireland (which went before the European Court of Human Rights) – to show how specific definitions of 'homosexual' acts and identities are invoked in law:

A distinction must be drawn between homosexuals who are such because of some kind of innate instinct or pathological constitution judged to be incurable and those whose tendency comes from a lack of normal sexual development or from a habit or from experience or from other similar causes but whose tendency is not incurable. (Judge Walsh, quoted in Moran, 1996, p. 176)

This introduces what Moran calls a 'dichotomy according to a logic of good and evil', of 'pervert-invert, acquired-congenital' (p. 177), offering human rights only to the 'good homosexual', the congenital invert, and demonizing others. The question of whether sexual identity is 'congenital' or 'acquired' has of course dogged the progress of lesbian and gay rights arguments, especially in law (see, for example, Currah, 1995; Halley, 1994). The controversial appearance of Simon LeVay's work on the so-called gay brain is only the latest chapter in the essentialism/constructionism debate, and will be by no means the last (LeVay, 1993, 1996; see also Rosario, 1997, and for a critical commentary on LeVay, see Hegarty, 1997). The curious appeal of gay brain research – in terms of validating (by essentializing) gay identity – reveals the yawning gap between queer theory's constructionist and performative accounts and the experiences of same-sex desire among many people (Tatchell, 1996). As John Weir (1996, pp. 32–3) provocatively formulates it: 'The true division in the gay community is between the entrenched, privileged, politically active urban and suburban trend-setters and policy makers, and the mass of people with homosexual urges who feel represented more by *Reader's Digest* and *Soldier of Fortune* magazine than by *The Advocate*'.

Weir's polemic introduces a widely voiced critique of queer politics as the politics of a metropolitan elite, unintelligible to the majority of 'people with homosexual urges'. The alignment of queer politics (and, as we have already seen, modes of AIDS activism) with so-called lifestyle politics has been used to suggest that it cannot have the same widespread appeal as the assimilationist agenda – an argument made particularly forcefully by gay conservatives, but also by what Rosaria Champagne (1998) calls '(anti-) queer Marxists' who wish to retain an old-school revolutionary struggle in the sphere of sexual politics. Outside the USA, there has been an added dimension to this tension, raising questions about the usefulness of queer politics, read as an American model of activism, in different political cultures. For example, histories of ACT UP chapters in Europe show the difficulties of importing modes of activism directly from the USA (Duyvendak, 1996). Moreover, Weir's provocation also demands that we attend to the question of class in relation to the question of sexual politics and sexual citizenship.

Queer with class

> The gay rights movement is crippled by a sense of entitlement... [It]
> is largely helmed by white men who crave what they were promised
> as children, but denied as adults because of their sexuality; they
> want guaranteed access to power. And they're not necessarily inter-
> ested in extending that power to you, just because you like having
> sex, sometimes, with guys. (Weir, 1996, p. 34)

As critical commentaries often note, there has been a relative
absence of class antagonism in recent lesbian and gay struggles.
The days of Gay Liberation have been left behind in favour of
assimilationist rights claims; despite the insistence of Nicola Field
(1995, p. 152) that 'class struggle and gay resistance are part of the
same battle', what we read in her account is instead a series of (as
she sees it) 'class betrayals' by the gay reformist lobby, by gay
businesses and by un-class-conscious lesbians and gay men. Alan
Sinfield similarly notes the demise of Gay Lib-style politics since the
1960s, but wants nonetheless to retain a left stance in the future
forms of sexual politics: 'some of that old-fashioned political stuff
needs to be kept going' (1998, p. 186). And Peter Cohen's (1997)
analysis of ACT UP New York's 'class style' vividly describes that
sense of entitlement to which Weir refers. Cohen quotes Michelangelo Signorile's statement that 'We're *from* the system' (p. 97) to
explain the unwillingness of groups like ACT UP to push for more
revolutionary change, and their adoption of accommodationist
'bourgeois militancy' instead. The shifting relationship between
(homo)sexual politics and class struggle is also captured in Donna
Minkowitz's lament at Clinton's inaugural ball: 'What had become
of our war with traditional values? Where were sexual freedom, the
critique of the family, and the memory of a group called the Gay
Liberation Front as we swayed to the Sousa played by a gay
marching band?' (1997, p. 23).

In the wake of the rise of gay conservativism and accommodationist or reformist rights-based politics – and of their incorporation
by the centre-left – Tony Kushner (1997, p. 185) asks the telling
question: 'Is there a relationship between homosexual liberation and
socialism?' Equally telling is his aside that '[t]hat's an unfashionably

utopian question'. And it's true that reading back through GLF manifestos in the cold light of postideological late modernity does make their clarion cries seem over-optimistically utopian. However, we might concur with José Esteban Muñoz (1996, p. 357), who writes that queer politics 'needs a real dose of utopianism', especially since 'utopia offers us a critique of the present, of *what is*, by casting a picture of what *can and perhaps will be*'. Materializing that utopia depends on the concrete political strategies and tactics deployed by sexual dissidents, as well as a vision of what goals might be set. As Tony Kushner asks: '[A]re officially sanctioned homosexual marriages and identifiably homosexual soldiers the ultimate aims of homosexual liberation? . . . [Or] are homosexual marriages and soldiery the ultimate, which is to say the only achievable, aims of the *gay rights movement*, a politics not of vision but of pragmatics?' (1997, p. 185; emphasis in original).

In the 'politics of pragmatics' we see particular notions of what kinds of action are necessary in order to further this rights agenda – which we will explore more fully in the next chapter. For other activists, such as Stonewall's Anya Palmer, the cornerstone of rights agitation is to get more people involved in a common struggle, and the key to that is visibility, which means coming out:

> Our role as activists will be to develop this re-involvement in politics – to inform and educate individual lesbians and gay men about the legal issues and social policies that affect all our lives. In part this will be achieved by simply encouraging greater visibility: *coming out, after twenty-five years of modern lesbian and gay politics, remains the central key to our liberation. Coming out, telling the truth about our lives, is still the most important contribution any of us can make.* (1995, pp. 49–50, emphasis ours)

The controversy over outing, of course, recasts this issue in a tension between (collective) visibility and (individual) privacy (Gross, 1993). And even coming out (never mind outing) is too much of a political tactic for some – especially gay conservatives – who see the answer to rights reform in complete assimilation. From their perspective, *passing* is the key to sexual citizenship. For accommodationist strategists, passing means that politics and identity can be disentangled: 'The concept of passing carries with it the assumption that one's acts, one's behaviour, even one's politics, can be split off from one's definition of self, that the self is not constructed in and through social practices' (Currah, 1995, pp. 66–7). It is crucial to recognize the danger inherent in such invisibilizing assimilation; the dream of a gay couple that nobody notices is gay, which Bruce Bawer would wish for, is the dream of the death of sexual politics. Against such a tendency, Anna Marie Smith (1997, p. 135) urges that '[t]his would be a good time indeed to learn from the wisdom of the uncompromising anti-assimilationist politics that developed within the most progressive moments of the anti-imperialist, civil rights, black power, sexual liberation, social feminist, lesbian feminist, and women of color feminist movements'.

This brings us back to queer politics. As Carl Stychin (1995, p. 141) describes it, queer politics offers novel forms of political alliance and agitation, since it insists upon a 'strategically articulated commonality forged from differently located subject positions'. While there are still strong and well-made criticisms of queer's supposed inclusiveness (and here, crucially, the issue of class returns), its 'in-your-face' interventions in the landscape of sexual citizenship certainly offer a radical alternative to the cosy assimilationism of gay conservatism. (A useful discussion of the tensions between essentialistic gay rights politics and constructionist queer politics, framed as offering respectively challenges to institutional and cultural oppression, is provided by Gamson (1996).) Writing in the heyday of queer politics, Cherry Smyth summed up the attractions it then seemed to offer:

> Queer promises a refusal to apologise or assimilate into invisibility. It provides a way of asserting desires that shatter gender identities and sexualities, in a manner some early Gay Power and lesbian feminist activists once envisaged. Perhaps it will fail to keep its promise, but its presence now in the early 90s marks the shape of the territory to come with an irrevocable and necessary passion. (1992, p. 60)

In the year 2000, echoing Smyth's premonition, it seems we are post-queer; at least that's implied in the tone of books fresh off the presses, such as Alan Sinfield's (1998) *Gay and After*: he discusses queer politics in the past tense, and suggests that its demise has been the result of its elitism – that it was only ever a politics of a

vanguard, who inevitably succumbed to fatigue once the movement failed to gain critical mass. Sinfield seems to propose in place
of either gay conservatism and assimilation or queer radicalism a
kind of post-gay 'third way': 'the task is not to imagine an exclusive
group of like-minded people, but to build on the diverse strengths of
our constituency, to enlarge it, and to politicise it' (p. 199). What
this seems to mean is accommodating some elements of assimilationism (in recognition that 'in-your-face' visibility is not an option
for everyone, and very much depends on material circumstances)
together with some of the principles of queer politics (inclusiveness
without homogeneity, the personal as political) – in much the same
way as proposed by Davina Cooper in *Power in Struggle*. As Joshua
Gamson (1996, p. 410) writes, finding this 'third way' is intensely
problematic, since it must resolve 'a fundamental quandary:...
clear identity categories are both necessary and dangerous distor-
tions, and moves to both fix and unfix them are reasonable'.

   In a tongue-in-cheek provocation that 'men who have sex with
men' might be the true sexual dissidents of our time (since they
resist identitarian restriction altogether), Sinfield (1998, p. 192)
notes that 'there are more ways than we normally allow of relating
to both conformity and transgression in the prevailing sex-gender
system and some of these ways have positive potential'. While this
is always going to seem like an uncomfortable compromise position,
in that it has to reconcile two apparently polar-opposite modalities,
the task for revisioning sexual citizenship must be to realize that
positive potential, and to imagine ways to critically disassemble
heteronormativity. The themes we trace through *The Sexual Citizen*
represent our attempt to intervene in this refiguring of sexual
citizenship; clearly that will be an on-going task, and it will inevitably encounter many obstacles along the way. What we would like
to echo is José Muñoz's (1996) call to revisit utopianism rather than
always treading the least-resistance path of the politics of pragmatics. And for us, that would seem to accord much more with
the imperatives of queer politics – no matter what its shortcomings
might be – than with the flight from politics found in the world of
Andrew Sullivan and his like-minds. As Muñoz says, such utopianism makes explicit the links between the 'desire for politics' and the
'politics of desire' (p. 371). Keeping sight of both seems the best
place to begin rethinking sexual citizenship.

3

Marriage, the Military and the Sexual Citizen

In the preceding chapters, we began to map out the formations of sexual citizenship that are the heart of this book. Here, we want to shift our focus and explore in more detail the ways in which (often contradictory) notions of sexual citizenship get mobilized around particular issues, debates and practices. Our focus is on the two most prominent arenas for rights claims by dissident sexual citizens in the UK and USA (but also in other nation-states, too): the right to marriage and the right to join the armed forces. While there has been a tendency to associate these agitations only with an assimilationist or gay conservative agenda (see, for example, Champagne, 1998), the lines of argument mobilized (both for and against) give us important insights into the logics of sexual citizenship in the context of rights claims.

Marrying into citizenship

> Whether marriage is normalizing or not for the individuals who marry, the debate about marriage has done much to normalize the gay movement.   (Warner, 1999, p. 143)

Arguments around same-sex marriage have come to take centre-stage in many lesbian and gay rights movements. In terms of sexual citizenship, marriage is often focused on as a necessary element of the politics of recognition – in this case, the recognition of same-sex union. The question is, of course, also one of equality: heterosexuals can marry, so it is wrong that lesbian and gay couples cannot enjoy the same privilege. Evan Wolfson (1996, p. 79), advancing the case for gay marriage in the USA, refers to wedlock as both a 'basic human right' and a 'constitutional freedom': 'Because literally hundreds of important legal, economic, practical, and social benefits and protections flow directly from marriage, . . . exclusion from this central social institution wreaks real harm on real-life same-sex couples every day' (p. 8).

This has been one of the principal focal-points of the agitations for the right to marry: that there are benefits enjoyed by married couples (health care, inheritance, insurance, etc.) that are denied to the unmarried. Moreover, marriage represents a public and state-sanctioned avowal of the couple's relationship and commitment. For Morris Kaplan, this means that steps like gay marriage must be the direction that lesbian and gay activism moves in: to work for full inclusion or recognition, since such strategies assert 'the positive status of lesbian and gay citizenship' – they represent the 'demands of queer families to enjoy equal social and legal status with their straight counterparts' (1997, p. 204). Crucially for Kaplan, lesbian and gay marriage is central to attaining full citizenship and empowerment, since it offers such recognition of the freedom of intimate association, insulated by law. As he concludes: 'Lesbian and gay marriages, domestic partnerships, and the reconceiving of family institutions as modes of intimate association among free and equal citizens all are efforts to appropriate, extend, and transform the available possibilities' (p. 222).

Against this line of argument, other writers in the USA stress that marrying into citizenship would have the opposite effect, closing down the 'available possibilities'; moreover, as Michael Warner says, marriage serves to reprivatize queer desires, pushing them back into the monogamous couple-form. The focus of so much rights agitation on the issue of marriage, he writes, also works as 'an increasingly powerful way of distracting citizens from the real, conflicted, and unequal conditions governing their lives' (Warner, 1999, p. 100). Nevertheless, the right to marry in the USA is conceived among liberal-reformist activists as the cornerstone for attaining full citizenship, given the centrality of marriage and the family to the notion of citizenship itself. Critiquing the pro-marriage lobby, Warner concludes that

> Discussions of gay marriage fall into characteristically American patterns of misrecognition; for example, the meaning of marriage is not social or institutional at all, but one of private commitment of two loving people; marriage has neither normative nor regulatory consequences, and is uncoercive because it simply fulfills the right to marry as a free individual choice; marriage means whatever people want it to mean; and so on.   (p. 133)

Outside of the USA, agitations for and against same-sex marriage reveal the importance of national political contexts. Henning Bech's modest but insightful 'Report from a rotten state' (1992), a commentary on the Danish registered partnership law passed in 1989, for example, distils the terms of debate among proponents and opponents of the law to show the extent to which political and legal questions get framed in particular, contextualized ways. In this case, both sides argued that their stand on the law was important to say something about *Denmark* (either to protect it from international ridicule or to position it at the forefront of civilization and human rights). The limits of the Danish law reform – omitting adoption rights and the right to a church wedding – were seen by some activists to have consolidated the status of homosexuals as second-class citizens, while also advocating a fixed model of homosexual relationships that denies an acceptance of their diversity. However, Bech notes that such an oppositional critique was relatively marginal to the public debate in Denmark. In a simliar vein, Angelia Wilson (1995) sketches a shift in British gay politics, from the GLF's revolutionary calls for the abolition of the family to present agitations based on the rhetorics of rights, justice and equality. In countries where some form of marriage or registered partnership is in place for same-sex couples, the reception has been very mixed, with some commentators arguing that marriage has led to the loss of significant elements of lesbian and gay culture and politics. Discussing the arguments in Germany, Judith Rauhofer (1998, p. 73) concludes that 'gay and lesbian politics that focus on merely sharing rights and privileges that come out of the heterocentric system deny themselves the opportunity to make a difference'.

In the USA, too, gay liberationists of the 1970s critiqued the elevation of the family, arguing that one task of gay liberation must be to broaden the opportunities for living outside the traditional heterosexual family – for gays and straights alike (D'Emilio, 1992). Most forcibly, John D'Emilio, writing at the start of the 1980s, urged the building of an 'affectional community' in which the family would become progressively insignificant for all members of society. The stark contrast between gay liberation's utopian social project (in which gay culture leads) and the 'pro-family' agenda of liberal reformism (where gay culture seeks to replicate heterosexual culture) is truly striking. By mainstreaming sexual politics, then, the radical edge is blunted and a 'back-door revolution' advocated, with things like partnership registration held as practical and strategic steps towards justice. Such moves tread a very fine line – which many of their advocates seem aware of, yet incapable of resolving – as well as revealing tensions within the agendas of different campaigning positions.

Opening up the question of lesbian and gay marriage, of course, *can* have far broader impacts, throwing light onto both the constructions of homosexuality and heterosexuality in law, and the limitations of such constructions. Dennis Allen's (1995) discussion of the public debate on same-sex marriage in Hawaii, in the light of a suit filed by two lesbian couples and one gay male couple (*Baehr* v. *Lewin*), clearly illustrates the destabilizing function of such appeals: as the Hawaii Supreme Court struggled to refine its definiton of 'marriage' (by linking it irrevocably to heterosexuality through the dubious logic of reproductive biologism, while also trying to sidestep sexual discrimination), it revealed 'the logical difficulties, the internal gaps and fissures, not only in the "inevitable" linking of marriage to heterosexuality but within the very idea of heterosexuality itself' (Allen, 1995, pp. 617–18). By having to draw a boundary around marriage defined in relation to reproduction, it excluded involuntarily childless heterosexual couples, and its tortuous attempts to bring them in (by reference to medical technology and the *potential* for reproduction) threatened to open a door for same-sex couples (who could equally use medical technologies to overcome biological barriers to reproduction). As with legal definitions of sodomy (in *Bowers* v. *Hardwick*, for example, where the Georgia law defined sodomy as oral or anal sex without explicitly demarcat-

ing the genders of participants), the precariousness of the homo/
hetero binary is exposed; in this case, it is heterosexuality that
comes to be defined by conduct – using a rather convoluted definition of 'natural' (or at least naturalized), *potential* reproductive
conduct. Such problematic defining of sexuality exposes the constructedness of categories in law.

It is this kind of exposure that advocates of registered partnerships
often point towards, and the 'broader agenda' behind such struggles
for reform; far from assimilationist, then, same-sex marriage is held
as capable of undermining the most solid of social structures ('the
family') by infiltrating it and exposing its contradictory logics from
within. The fact that the take-up rate for registered partnerships in
Denmark has been very low is thus of only secondary importance
when set alongside the bigger picture of both the *possibility* of partnership registration for those who may want it, and the *threat* to
marriage that registered partnerships purportedly pose.

Marriage rites and rights

This seems to be the currently dominant political methodology
expressed in both academic and activist discourses: the 'quest for
justice' within the broad equal rights/citizenship framework, with
the suggestion that riding on the back of these claims are more
troublesome 'hidden agendas' – of challenging structural homophobia and thereby questioning the foundational definitions of
sexual citizenship. *Bowers* v. *Hardwick*, for example, challenged
Georgia's sodomy laws through the lens of the right to privacy,
while also navigating an uneasy path through the relation of
homosexual identity to homosexual conduct. The framing of the
challenge within rights discourse, which occupies a particular and
sensitive place within American law and culture, opened up the
terms of the debate in more far-reaching ways, by raising questions
about the immutability (or mutability) of homosexual identity
(whether or not sexuality is legally analogous to 'race', thus opening up its eligibility for shelter under the Equal Protection Amendment) and about the extent of overlap between 'homosexual
conduct' and 'homosexual identity'. The question remains, however, of whether reducing radical activism to claims under law has

a positive impact. As Nan D. Hunter (1995b, p. 120) says, for advocates of legal approaches, 'the process of organizing and litigating empowers and emboldens', while for its critics 'the reduction of radical demands into claims of "rights under the law" perpetuates belief systems that teach that other, more transformative modes of change are impossible, unnecessary, or both'.

It is worth examining in more detail the logic of this methodology – and the argument over legal-reformist versus 'radical' action – through the debate on same-sex marriage, since advocates are keen to stress the subversive challenge posed by what can be read as an assimilationist strategy. As Hunter (1995c) points out, the politics of the family have increasingly become an arena of social combat central to agitations for lesbian and gay equality and citizenship. In a sense, marriage is a useful cypher for the whole citizenship debate, since it is seen as a cohesive element of social life, straddling the public and the private, containing a mix of rights and duties, and occupying a central position in political, legal and popular discourses of radically different orientations – from the petitions for the recognition of 'families we choose' to campaigns for a reinstatement of 'family values' as the heart of Christian-democratic political and moral culture. Agitation in the USA for the rights of 'queer families' enables us to witness these competing discourses enacted on the political and legal stage. Hunter suggests that same-sex marriage could potentially transform the institution of marriage in its current form, also sending out shockwaves that may shake the foundations of other social institutions that are presently loci of discrimination. Part of Hunter's argument rests with the potential of same-sex marriage to destabilize the gendered structure of marriage, fracturing discourses of dependency and authority. It serves, then, to *denaturalize* marriage, to reveal its constructedness, and thereby to 'democratize' it.

Paradoxically, however, it seems that such a move could have the function of *reaffirming* marriage as an institution. There are a number of strands to this counterargument. First, by further marginalizing the unmarried, it perpetuates a two-tier system in the recognition of relationship status. It also maintains the (long-term, monogamous) bonds of coupledom as the most legitimate form of lovelife-choice (Card, 1996). It 'liberalizes' the institution of marriage, opening it up to those (heterosexual) people who currently oppose its inequalities, as well as comforting those married couples currently uneasy about their privileged status – again reinforcing (and relegitimizing) marriage over and above non-married relationships. It puts people currently ineligible to marry under increased moral and legal pressure to wed (such as homosexual couples with children). Meanwhile, it fails to address economic aspects of marriage (whether positive, such as tax breaks, or negative, in terms of welfare and dependency); nor does it address the continuing links between marital status and other forms of legal rights (next of kin status, intestate inheritance, etc.).

Perhaps most significantly, it upholds the notions of a particular model of romantic love and commitment, which in many ways are more central to the meaning of marriage than (potentially) procreative coupling, at least outside of legal discourses. A focus exclusively on challenging the legal discourse around marriage, therefore, falls short of considering which aspects of *popular discourse* are contested or reaffirmed by such a move. Since popular discourses then spill over into political and legal process (the recent British moral panic over single mothers, for example), strategies for change need to consider the many meanings of marriage (and non-marriage) that contribute to its social (as well as legal) status. As Katherine O'Donovan (1993, p. 87) rightly suggests, marriage retains such an iconic status in society that it is almost inconceivable to think outside its logics: 'There is a kind of uniform monotony to our fates. We are destined to marry or to enter similar relationships'. From this perspective, demanding the right to join that uniform monotony starts to look like a strange political tactic for sexual dissidents. We take up this theme in chapter 7.

Hunter, meanwhile, reviews calls for same-sex marriage law alongside the alternative strategy of registered partnership legislation, in part examining feminist arguments around both, as well as critiquing work from critical legal studies that has focused on questioning the use of rights discourse in such mobilizations. Registered partnerships offer many practical advantages (and are not hidebound by 'tradition' to construct contractual obligations along marriage-like lines), but lack the status (in both legal and cultural senses) of marriage; unless marriage is abolished altogether and replaced by a single system of partnership registration, that distinction will remain, and will carry with it ideological and moral weight (Wolfson, 1996). Further, as Claudia Card (1996) notes, the requirement in registered partnerships that the couple shares living space can make it a more restrictive arrangement than marriage.

As we have already noted, an important part of the pro-marriage argument rests on the economic benefits currently not available to non-married partners. However, arguing that marriage will necessarily bring economic benefits for lesbian and gay couples denies the fact that many marriages are relationships of economic dependency (Van Every, 1992). Moreover, there is a class politics at work here. As Eva Pendleton (1996) says, the main proponents of same-sex marriage in the USA are dual-income, middle-class white gay men. So, while Evan Wolfson (1996, p. 82) argues that the right to marry is a fight whose 'stakes cut across race, gender, and class lines', Victoria Brownworth (1996, p. 96) reminds us that 'for generations in the United States, the married state has been associated with class: poor white trash don't get married; they just "shack up" together'.

One aspect of lesbian and gay marriage that is not often considered in discussions is the so-called mutually beneficial arrangement – the marriage between a lesbian and a gay man for strategic reasons (often immigration status). While this is often portrayed as a desperate (not to mention dangerous) move, such 'marriages of convenience' could be seen as offering a further, more transgressive strategy. If gay men married lesbians *en masse* as a *political act*, then the status of marriage as the state-licensed public statement of romantic love and life-long commitment would be exposed and undermined. The couple would have a claim on all the benefits of marriage without having to bear the responsibilities, while also falling completely outside current discourses of what marriage means (or *should* mean).[1]

The strategic claiming of the right of same-sex couples to marry also runs the risk of domesticating sexual practice, lending support to policies that seek to 'clean up' tabooed aspects of gay culture (principally public sex) as well as distancing 'assimilationist' agitation from radical activism. As Eva Pendleton suggests, the assimilationist agenda in American gay politics has a profoundly conservative orientation:

> These boys are anxious to recoup the white, middle-class privilege that has previously been denied to openly gay men. Rather than challenge this hegemony, they will do what they can to overcome

the political handicap that homosexuality has traditionally represented. The best way to do this, they argue, is to assimilate into
Middle America as much as possible.   (1996, p. 375)

Such a position leads, in Pendleton's eyes, to desexualized political
activism; her reading of gay conservative texts such as Bruce
Bawer's *A Place at the Table* (1993) uncovers the erotophobia
inherent in demands for same-sex marriage. Public sex is especially
demonized as a *political* practice (in fact, its politics are erased under
the trope of hedonism and irresponsibility). Bawer's take on gay
marriage, as outlined by Pendleton, is to suggest that granting
lesbians and gay men the right to marry will help preserve heterosexual marriage, in part by ending the 'sham marriages' that
closeted lesbians and gay men enter into. What this exposes is
precisely the dangers that assimilationist strategies are prone to:
their recuperation by conservative agendas and agenda-setters.
Activism based on rights agitation – especially around issues such
as partnership/marriage or the right to privacy – can serve to erase
aspects of sexual citizenship founded outside the narrow bounds of
normalcy, again illustrating the tension between definitions of the
'good homosexual' and the 'bad homosexual', erasing the possibility of queer counterpublics, and instating passing as the modality of
citizen-behaviour for queers. Pendleton is at pains to point out,
however, that many radical (non-conservative) agitations also
valorize monogamy as the 'responsible' mode of sexual citizenship
in the time of AIDS. Pervasive sex-negativity can only be further
enabled by demands for the right to marry as long as marriage and
monogamy remain shackled together. Given the force of these kinds
of argument, it seems unlikely that marriage will advance the cause
of dissident sexual citizens in any direction other than assimilation.
As Claudia Card (1996, p. 9) puts it, 'we need better traditions'.

Army of lovers

Nearly everyone who supports the 'ideal' of same-sex marriage also
believes strongly that lesbians and gay men should be able to serve
openly in the military. And for the last 5 years, these two issues
have been the primary focus of the entire lesbian and gay civil

rights movement, superseding even concerns over the AIDS epidemic.   (Brownworth, 1996, p. 94)

A second – and in many ways related – focus of arguments for
reform in the realm of contemporary sexual citizenship, then, has
been the ban of homosexuality (or, more properly, of homosexuals)
within the armed forces. The gays in the military debate in the USA
can similarly be seen to instate *passing* as the only possible strategy
for homosexuals serving in the forces, since any form of homosexual conduct (including coming out) contravenes the Defense
Department's policy: 'The identity/conduct distinction that advocates for gay, lesbian and bisexual rights have been so eager to assert
is collapsed, in this instance through the mediating category of
speech: homosexuality is articulated through speech, and speech
has been summarily defined, by the courts, and by the Clinton
administration, as conduct' (Currah, 1995, p. 66).

Even withholding homosexual identity – by passing – can, however, be used as grounds for dismissal. In fact, in a landmark US
case, *Steffan* v. *Cheney*, the full force of the Department of Defense's
homophobia apparently centred on the very act of passing:

> Steffan was under a positive *duty* as a member of the military to
> come out because his gay identity was otherwise undetectable but
> contrary to regulations. The result of his coming out, though, was
> his expulsion as unfit for service. Paradoxically, however, in going
> public he revealed that his sexuality had not rendered him incapable
> of service. He demonstrated, instead, that absent a public declara-
> tion, he remained completely undetectable on the inside of what is,
> in the end, an institution forged with same-sex bonds   (Stychin,
> 1995, p. 94)

Steffan's presence in the navy thus threatened to destabilize (or at
least muddy) the distinction between a sanctioned homosociality
and an outlawed homosexuality – a distinction actually very precariously enacted in institutions like the military, Stychin argues.
The navy's fear, put simply, is of *contagion* (backed up by arguments
upholding Steffan's expulsion centred on the 'threat' of HIV and
AIDS impacting on the 'healthy' military's abilities to defend the
nation): 'the sexual subject, the national subject and the healthy

subject all come to be assimilated with each other and Joseph Steffan . . . is constructed as foreign to any and all of these subjectivities' (p. 99). Paradoxically, then, as Stychin notes:

> Joseph Steffan was defined as an outsider because of his ability to pass – to reveal, through the articulation of a gay identity, that he was an insider all along. However, in assimilating the military with the nation, Steffan is further constructed, not as *being* an insider but as performing the role of the insider – as an espionage agent might perform a role to undermine national security. The underlying concern, then, is not simply that Steffan had successfully performed the role until his own revelation, but that his success had revealed the performativity of the military subject. (p. 99)

The need for state agencies like the military to purge themselves of the 'homosexual menace', described by Nan Hunter (1995a) as the McCarthyism of the 1980s, is, of course, by no means new. In the UK, too, the 'enemy within' – which shifted between communism and forms of 'character defect' (including homosexuality) – has a long association with questions of national security. As Les Moran (1991) points out, however, it is inaccurate to assume a straightforward and constant construction of homosexuality as necessarily constituting a security risk. Focusing on the British intelligence agencies, Moran shows that links between sexual identity and breaches of national security, as in the cases of spies like Anthony Blunt and Guy Burgess, have not always been deployed in demonizing 'traitors'. The social position of intelligence agents as members of an elite, Moran argues, allowed for discretion in matters of sexuality, as long as it remained 'invisible'. McCarthyism's enthusiastic binding together of communism, homosexuality and national threat, however, was imported into the UK in the 1950s as international relations between the UK and USA took centrestage in the political climate of the cold war, serving to solidify the equation of homosexuality with risks to national security on both sides of the Atlantic.

Hunter sketches a similar postwar history of this shifting process in the USA, from the demonizing of homosexuals as subversives capable of destroying the state during the cold war witch-hunts right up to the 'no homo promo' stand coming out of the Briggs Initiative (an attempt to outlaw the 'advocating of homosexuality' in schools) and its later relations, such as the Helms Amendment

(attacking sex-positive HIV and AIDS health promotion material) –
all of which come to cluster around the question of what Hunter
calls 'sexual identity speech', – moving away from conduct to
expression as outlawed action (see also Duggan, 1995). What the
gays in the military issue also makes clear, Hunter points out, is the
complex intertwining of privacy, equality and expression central to
current forms of sexual citizenship agitation (and to its regulation).
In order to prohibit the 'public' statement (confession or coming-
out) of homosexuality by serving military personnel, the military
must itself repeatedly speak the term – generating more of the 'sex
talk' that Cooper (1993a) identifies as central to the act of making
things public so as to render them private; this means constructing
a 'homosexual military subject' in order to deny her or his existence. In Judith Butler's (1997a, p. 104) words, '[t]he regulation
must conjure one who defines him or herself as a homosexual in
order to make plain that no such self-definition is permissible within
the military'; the definition of homosexuality must always come
from outside (from the state, the law or the military), never from
inside. The debate becomes about not gays in the military, but what
Butler calls 'gay speech in the military'.

The US military's 'Don't ask, don't tell' ruling, however, offers a
strange opt-out clause, or 'rebuttal presumption' – the possibility of
renunciation by unchaining identity from conduct ('I am a homosexual and I intend not to act on my desire'), or the possibility of
writing off an isolated incident of 'homosexual conduct' as a 'mistake'. Reading this rebuttal presumption psychoanalytically, Butler
concludes:

> The renunciation by which the military citizen is purged of his [or
> her] sin and reestablished in his or her place, then, becomes the act
> by which the prohibition at once denies and concedes homosexual
> desire; it is not, strictly speaking, *un*speakable, but is, more generally,
> retained in the speaking of the prohibition. In the case of the homo-
> sexual who claims to be one, but insists that he or she will not act on
> his or her desire, the homosexuality persists in and as the application
> of that prohibiton to oneself.   (1997a, pp. 117–18).

For Butler, this logic throws into relief the very issue of citizenship's
relationship to homosexuality: the 'military citizen' exists in a twi-

light zone of citizenship – similar to the ambivalent status of immigrants, oscillating between legal and illegal, as well as inhabiting the interstices of (il)legality. The military citizen thus reminds us of the necessary disavowal of homosexuality in citizenship: homosexuality must be commuted to non-erotic homosociality, in order to desexualize the social bonds between service personnel, as it must between citizens (McGhee, 1998).

These kinds of reading of the US ban on gays in the military help us to understand the complexities inherent in legal-political discourses – they do the same work as Allen's reading of *Baehr* v. *Lewin*. But we should remember, yet again, that there is also a material dimension to consider. Being thrown out of the military for being gay may serve to reveal the military's fragile discursive hold on the homosexual/heterosexual binary, and its equally fragile conception of the relationship between conduct and identity – but that doesn't help those service personnel dismissed. And here, once more, there is an important class component to bear in mind. For many working-class queers, the military has long been the only available way of escaping an oppressive homelife; moreover, as Claudia Card (1996) points out, many people from low-income backgrounds enlist in order to receive the educational and other benefits otherwise denied them. So, while some lesbian and gay activists argue that the very fact that 'straight-acting' gay men and lesbians can successfully pass in the armed forces and thereby gain those benefits makes the unbanning lobby politically suspect, others make the argument that queering the military would destabilize an institution which, like marriage, has for too long rested on heterosexual privilege, and thereby destabilize heterosexuality itself (McGhee, 1998; Stychin, 1996). Of course, there are also those who argue that queers shouldn't want to join up in the first place – that the military is oppressive and heteropatriarchal (just like the family). As Brownworth (1996, p. 95) puts it, marriage and the military are both 'inherently *anti*-queer'.

Soldiers, spouses, citizens

Our purpose in this chapter has been to think about the ways in which the debates on same-sex marriage and gays in the military are debates about sexual citizenship. Certainly, for advocates of both causes, the denial of the right to fight or marry marks sexual dissidents as second-class citizens. As we hope to have shown, whatever your take on the debates, the way in which arguments get framed inevitably brings into relief the formulations of citizenship and rights that sexual politics has to work with currently. In effect, the lifting of the ban on lesbians and gay men openly serving in the armed forces may produce an outcome like that described by Henning Bech in his 'Report from a rotten state' – heralded as a symbolic victory for sexual dissidents, the actual possibility of registered partnerships in Denmark has not radically shifted the landscape of sexual citizenship. We might be able to take it as a barometer of tolerance, a recognition of diversity. But we have to be mindful, as Michael Warner urges us, to look at what's lost as well as what's gained. That's why Claudia Card argues it is possible to support the unbanning of gays in the military without coupling that with support for gay marriage; both are indexes of sexual citizenship, to be sure; but they produce markedly different outcomes – in reality as well as in theory. Crucially, as we hope we have made clear, there are different agendas for class politics in each case. In that way, the debates serve as a useful case-study for rethinking the project of rights-claims as the central thrust of sexual citizenship.

4

The Sexual and the Social

The notion of the social/sexual split is a sexualised notion, establishing heterosexuals as a socially inscribed class and lesbians and
gay men as a sexually inscribed grouping.

Diane Richardson, 'Heterosexuality and social theory'

From our discussions of citizenship in the first three chapters, it
should be apparent that we consider all citizenship to be sexual
citizenship, as citizenship is inseparable from identity, and sexuality
is central to identity. Yet as we have noted, sexuality is often
omitted from discussions of citizenship in social theory. This is no
coincidence, as sexuality is commonly seen as outside of the social,
and as irrelevant to the formulations of social theory: 'Social theory
[has] an endless capacity to marginalize queer sexuality in its
descriptions of the social world' (Warner, 1993, p. ix). In this
chapter we want to argue that in order to advance the debate on
sexual citizenship we need to examine the ways in which the
separation of the sexual and the social is mobilized, before moving
on to explore different ways of conceptualizing the relationship
between the two. Recent debates between Judith Butler, Nancy
Fraser and Iris Marion Young on the politics of recognition and
redistribution show the different ways in which sexuality is positioned in the context of cultural politics – and how this is read in
relation to social and economic inequalities and injustices. While
sexuality has been brought into these debates, there has been very

little consideration of the erotic in this context. This leads us to ask a couple of crucial questions: What are the links between sociality, eroticism and solidarity? How can the erotic inform notions of the social? Finally we examine the spatial dimension in sexual politics, in order to explore the ways in which social exclusion from (sexual) citizenship is constituted through exclusion in space. But we shall begin in the space of the academy, by considering the debates about social theory and cultural politics.

What we mean when we speak about 'the social'

At one level, we can sketch the tension we are interested in here as one between the social and the cultural. In academic terms, this is manifest in the split between social theory and cultural studies. For example, cultural studies has come under attack for failing to address questions of redistribution and the inequalities of global capitalism, with some authors arguing that cultural studies is complicit in the continued domination of the capitalist mode of production. In *At Home in the World*, for example, Timothy Brennan (1997) berates cosmopolitan critics and intellectuals for their uncritical discussions of global culture – discussions that fail to address the social and economic inequalities of global capitalism. And, writing in the *New Left Review*, Slavoj Žižek argues that

> critical energy has found a basic substitute outlet in fighting for cultural differences which leave the basic homogeneity of the capitalist world system intact. So we are fighting our PC battles for the rights of ethnic minorities, of gays and lesbians, of different life-styles, and so on, which, in the guise of 'cultural studies', is doing the ultimate service to the unrestrained development of capitalism by actively participating in the ideological effort to render its massive presence invisible: in atypical postmodern 'cultural criticism', the very mention of capitalism as world system tends to give rise to the accusation of 'essentialism', 'fundamentalism' and other crimes.   (1997, p. 46)

Arguments such as Žižek's, which stress the degree to which social and economic inequalities have been evacuated in cultural criticism, serve to trivialize the significance of homophobia as a site of social and economic injustice – it's just a diverting 'PC battle'. Added to this is the problematic relationship between left politics and sexual politics. The left has long been suspicious of sex in general, and of dissident sexualities in particular. Andrew Parker (1993, p. 19) argues that 'Western Marxism's constitutive dependence on the category of production derives in part from an antitheatricalism, an aversion to certain forms of parody that prevents sexuality from attaining the political significance that class long monopolized.' When it does attempt to deal with sexual difference, the left seems capable of responding only in a paternal or maternal manner – affording legislative protection to the rights of lesbians and gay men thought of as victims who need the protection *of* the state, not *from* the state.

There is, then, a real tension here between the *politics of the social* (with their associated emphasis on rights and liberation through legislation) and *cultural politics* (with the stress on physical pleasures and desire) – and this has become instituted in academic theories as well as in the strategies of activists. At the same time, a number of writers in lesbian and gay studies and queer theory have expressed alarm at the degree to which the social (and the economic) has been marginalized within queer theory, which is argued to have shifted its focus onto the subjective meaning of sexuality (as we have already seen, for example, in the ways in which transgression is figured by Jeffrey Weeks) and away from the social (Warner, 1993). For us, this raises key questions that we want to explore in this chapter: How can one separate the subjective meaning of sexuality from any discussions of the social, for are they not intrinsically linked? What do we mean by the terms 'social' and 'cultural' – terms that are currently set in opposition to one another?

Socialist feminist writers, among others, have argued that queer theory is politically irresponsible in celebrating transgression to the neglect of material inequalities. For Rosemary Hennessy (1993), an emphasis on sexuality as erotic play is one of the main defining (and limiting) characteristics of queer theory and queer politics; she argues that as queer politics is steeped in postmodernist thinking, it can conceive of difference only as *cultural* rather than *social*: 'Difference as discursively constructed is invariably presented as exclusively cultural. One of the issues at stake here is queer theory's implicit conception of the social. Although it draws upon a range of critical frameworks, the social is consistently conceptualized as only a matter of representation, of discourse or symbolic relations' (p. 968).

The argument that the social is only a 'matter of representation' in queer theory misses the point that representations and social power are inextricably linked, and that modes of representation are both informed by and themselves inform the ways in which groups are treated in real life (Dyer, 1993) – to argue that sexual identities are the product of discourse does not mean that this does not have material consequences. In a sense, then, the distinction between the social and the cultural, or between the politics of redistribution and the politics of representation, is an oversimplified and outmoded distinction to make. The realms are, in fact, complexly intertwined, in that economic capital is inseparable from social, cultural and symbolic capital in structuring and sustaining patterns of inequality and injustice (Isin and Wood, 1999). The recent debates between Butler, Fraser and Young illustrate very well the continuing problem of resolving the designation of sexual politics as outside of the social, as *merely cultural*.

Merely cultural?

The current tendency in social theory to belittle the oppression of lesbians and gay men as 'merely cultural' has been taken to task by Judith Butler (1997b) in a recent exchange with Nancy Fraser (1997) in *Social Text*. Butler berates some Marxist critics for their continued attack on cultural politics. Centring her argument around queer politics, Butler (1997b, p. 270) notes that '[w]hereas class and race struggles are understood as pervasively economic, and feminist struggles to be sometimes economic and sometimes cultural, queer struggles are understood not only to be cultural struggles, but to typify the "merely cultural" form that contemporary social movements have assumed'. We are supportive of Butler's trenchant defence of queer struggles, and feel that we need to move beyond a proscriptive and antagonistic debate that produces the social as clearly distinct from the cultural.

What is particularly problematic is the notion that struggles for lesbian and gay rights do not have a material dimension – that the right to claim an identity is purely symbolic. Moreover, the view that lesbian and gay struggles are 'merely cultural' reinforces the commonly held (and homophobic) assumption that lesbians and gay men are an affluent group in society not in need of redistributive politics. Barbara Smith (1993) and Nancy Fraser (1997), for example, have both suggested that there is no *necessary relation* between homophobia and capitalism. Smith argues that racism has been the underlying structural basis of American capitalism, not homophobia, while Fraser points towards the strength of the pink economy as the basis for her claim that capitalism can successfully assimilate and accommodate gay interests. As Iris Marion Young (1997) notes in her intervention into this debate, Fraser's formulation, which maintains a dichotomy between political economy and culture – and of feminist, anti-racist and gay politics as fighting for recognition as an end in itself – downplays the fight for cultural recognition as an essential component of the struggle for economic, social and political justice. As we have already argued, the realms are co-implicated and connected in a way that Fraser's simplistic argument overlooks.

The distinction between the politics of recognition and the politics of redistribution is divisive, argues Young, because it ignores those who, for example, suffer materially *because of their identity*. Poverty makes invisible the experiences of socially marginalized lesbians and gay men, whose social and economic condition serves to reinforce isolation and exclusion from the urban commercial scenes that represent the most visible and intelligible manifestations of gay culture to the straight onlooker. The extent to which lesbian and gay commercial spaces are misrecognized and seen as representative of all lesbians and gay men as a uniformly affluent and economically privileged group in society serves to deny the material impacts of homophobia (in the workplace, for example) and the economic constraints that deny universal access to those spaces. Clearly, then, sexual politics are not 'merely cultural'; the task of the rest of this chapter is to explore the *social* dimensions of sexuality. Taking up Michael Warner's call in *Fear of a Queer Planet* (1993) to reinstate the social in queer theory, we want to think about ways in which the social is imagined as 'a new hybrid form of the public and the private', which thus produces 'a novel interlacing of interventions and withdrawals of the state' (Deleuze, 1979, p. x).

Socializing the sexual, queering the social?

In *Outside Belongings*, Elspeth Probyn (1996) argues that it is unhelpful to set the social and cultural in opposition to one another, insisting that we need instead to *widen* our conceptions of the social. Moreover, she places sexuality at the intersection of the two realms, and stresses that we need both to socialize the sexual and sexualize the social. She suggests a bold, speculative *queer imagining of the social*, which is sensitive to queer difference but also attuned to the social basis that enables the production of queer identities in the first place. She stresses that not all writing produced under the sign of queer theory needs protecting from the criticism that it lacks a social dimension, and that social and queer should not be seen in opposition to one another. In any reassertion of the social (as proposed, for example, by Seidman and Nicholson, 1995), it is crucial that sexuality is not overlooked (as has so often been the case in mainstream discussions of the social and the political); it is similarly important that sexual politics addresses issues of social inequality. For Probyn this does not merely mean a call for the inclusion of queer perspectives and voices into mainstream accounts of the social, but also an interrogation of the many ways in which sexuality and power are implicated in all our social arrangements: 'Rendering politics, the social, and the sexual relevant requires that we encourage interconnections, not further compartmentalization' (1996, p. 144).

Writers trying to develop queer articulations of the social, such as Lauren Berlant, maintain that discussions of sexual politics (what she labels 'intimacy crises') are normally marginalized within theorizations of the social:

> many radical social theorists see the political deployment of intimacy crises as merely ornamental or a distraction from 'real' politics.... [T]hey have been misdirected by a false distinction between the merely personal and the profoundly structural. These forms of sociality too often appear to be in separate worlds of analysis and commitment, with catastrophic political consequences for critical engagement with the material conditions of citizenship. (1997, p. 9)

However, she also recognizes the ever-present possibility for the assimilation of queer politics into mainstream capitalist culture, echoing Hennessy's argument. Berlant notes that the hegemonic conservatism of US politics means that claims for rights in the USA are forcefully made through consumption – including queer consumption. The economic dynamism of minority groups in the USA is used as evidence of the ability of these groups to assimilate and become 'proper' US citizens. Thus institutions such as gay marriage and consumption practices associated with the pink economy become symbols of how sexual minority groups obtain power in a society based on the market. As we have already seen, this leads to the mobilizing of particular and exclusionary forms of sexual citizenship that marginalize those who are socially excluded and economically disadvantaged.

These debates point towards the need for a clearer discussion of the place of the sexual in the social, and for a queer *production* of sociality (more than a queer *reading* of the social). It could be concluded from the discussion above that 'homosexual' stands opposite to the 'social' and 'society'. However, a number of writers have argued that homosexuality is in fact *central* to the social and to definitions of society. Below we want to look at the treatment of the social in the work of Guy Hocquenghem, Henning Bech and William Haver, who each have very different views on the centrality of the (homo)sexual to definitions of the social, and of society.

Homosocial theory

In Hocquenghem's *Homosexual Desire*, originally published in 1972, capitalism is argued to subjugate homosexuality because it threatens the social cohesion necessary for the reproduction of the capitalist mode of production:

> Capitalist society can only organise its relationships around the jealousy-competition system by means of the dual action of repression and sublimation of homosexuality; one underwrites the competitive rule of the phallus, the other the hypocrisy of human relationships. The phallocentric competitive society is based on the

> repression of desires directed at the anus; the repression of homo-
> sexuality is directly related to the jealousy paranoia that constitutes
> the daily fabric of society, and to the ideology of an integral social
> whole, the 'human community' we live in.   (1993, p. 105)

For Hocquenghem, this logic makes the homosexual an outsider in
society; homosexual desire threatens the social norm, as the production of society is predicated on the denial and repression of
homosexual desire. Hocquenghem also argues that homosexuality
is connected with surplus, with waste – as opposed to the world of
heterosexuality, which is equated with production (and reproduction): homosexuals are wasteful, and this undermines the produc-
tivity of modern capitalism.

Hocquenghem's thesis pre-supposes that our society necessarily
represses homosexual desire in order to preserve a social fabric
founded on de-eroticized homosociality; other writers, however,
have suggested that late capitalism actively mobilizes homosexuality. In late capitalism, the shift from production to consumption
has meant a seachange in the status of homosexuals, who are
equated with consumption and thereby now seen as socially useful
in terms of promoting consumption (Lowe, 1995). As Linda Singer
notes:

> capitalism works not only by opposing itself to the pleasure principle,
> but by finding strategic ways to mobilize it; a form of control by
> incitement, not by the repression but by the perpetual promise of
> pleasure, i.e., of that which is denied by the profit-producing process
> ... As a consequence of its success, late capitalism has largely suc-
> ceeded in establishing the articulation of needs and desires along two
> basic axes – genital gratification and satisfaction through consump-
> tion.   (1993, p. 37)

Against this surplus, this wastefulness, of course, is set the productive social unit of the family, which therefore becomes the bedrock
for social policy formulations, since it is seen as the bedrock of
society itself. Falling into a familial mode of citizenship – through
marriage, for example – or settling for consumer-citizenship status
by maintaining the myth of the pink economy, would seem the only
ways to counter the pervasive structuring of homosexuality as
surplus to society in Hocquenghem's reading of the sexual logic of

capitalism. Elsewhere, however, we find arguments that locate homosexuality very differently in its relation to the social.

The homosexual form of existence as social

In his astonishing study of the relationship between male homosexuality and modernity, *When Men Meet*, Henning Bech argues that the (male) homosexual is by definition a social creature – that modern homosexual identity always involves processes of socialization. He writes, moreover, that there is a particular *homosexual form of existence* or *social world*, with separate social norms and values, distinct from 'society as a whole'. For Bech, this form of existence is 'essentially social: it involves a relation to others one feels one resembles more or less, with whom one interacts, with whom one exchanges experiences and views' (1997, p. 154). As we shall see in the next chapter, this social world is, for Bech, an urban world: the city is the social stage on which the homosexual builds his social life.

Whatever one may think about the simplicity of Bech's definition of a single, uniform homosexual form of existence – whom we can identify as 'the homosexual' of whom he writes, and who might be for a variety of reasons excluded from his formulation – his work clearly points towards a queer conception of the social, placing the homosexual as central to the social. He notes, for example, that queer spaces demand a certain kind of socialization, that there are modes of being homosexual that must be acquired. Just as Bech argues that a gay identity demands socialization, Michael Warner notes that 'Queers do a kind of practical social reflection just in finding ways of being queer' (1993, p. xiii). Further, Bech suggests that, while homosexuals are represented as being outsiders in straight society, lesbians and gay men create their own social worlds, in separate spaces, with their own separate rituals and customs – all of which Bech celebrates as being liberatory. The problem with Bech's writing here is his exclusivity, as we have already noted: many queers find themselves excluded from the very social world that he portrays. Nevertheless, what Bech offers us in *When Men Meet* is a unique way of imagining the intimate links between the (homo)sexual and the social, which finds echoes in work we talk about in this book (especially Berlant and Warner, 1998; Muñoz, 1996). Importantly for us, Bech signals throughout his work the centrality of eroticism to this social world, and simultaneously the sociality of eroticism.

Sociality, eroticism, solidarity

In thinking through the place of sexuality in social theory, Michael Warner (1993) notes the legacy of Eve Sedgwick's (1985, 1990) work on the homosocial/homosexual distinction. For Sedgwick the denial of eroticism between men is consitutive of (homo)sociality – as we have already seen, for example, in Hocquenghem's argument that capitalist society rests on the repression of homo-eroticism. Closing down eroticism by commuting it into the homosocial bonding of citizens serves, therefore, to expel the erotic from the social – in effect, this is analogous to the expulsion of eroticism from the public sphere. However, Bech's discussion of the homosexual form of existence stresses the social dimension of homo-eroticism, writing the city as erotic social space.

Other writers have sought to expand the kinds of idea that we've traced in Bech's work, and to develop arguments about the social and the sexual dimensions of power. William Haver produces one imaginative way of treating the social in *The Body of this Death*. He argues that the queer (among others) is produced out of the very need to constitute the society of the normal – what he terms 'the privileged community of the Same':

> a certain social surplus – the IV drug user, the person of color, the sex worker, the queer – is produced in order to maintain humanism's 'society,' constituted in the genetic, viral, and bacteriological law and order of the clean and proper body, as *the* privileged community of the Same ... this so-called social surplus is not merely the index of the proliferation of objects before the panoptic Gaze of a magisterial transcendental subjectivity (the social scientist-engineer): much more radically, it is the endless proliferation, in destitution, of difference itself, signifying the radical impossibility of constituting 'society' as totality.

If the objectification of the social constructs a putative totality called 'society' and the historicization of the Real consists of a domination of meaning, taken together they are unavoidably and originarily a transcendental *forgetting* of the erotic, destitute, materiality of the Real in its historicity. (Haver, 1996, pp. 19–20)

Arguing that the queer is a *social* surplus is qualitatively different from arguing that homosexual desire represents a threat to a society; Hocquenghem's thesis presupposes that there is a stable entity named society which is threatened by homosexual desire, whereas Haver suggests that society is itself profoundly unstable, and needs to constantly repeat the process of reproducing itself. It is in the attempt to produce itself as a totalizing entity that society has to make invisible the erotic basis of its existence. The crux of Haver's argument comes with his exhilarating definition of the social as a lure:

Nonreserve, indeterminacy, sociality: these are not predicates, attributes, or qualities that would adhere to or inhere in an object, 'society,' for example. They are, rather, being-in-common itself. The question of the social is therefore not a matter of a dialectic of universal and particular; it is not a question of the *identity* of the particular or the identities of multiple particularities in relation to one another; for, however complex the sophistications of such relations, the particular is, as the particular *of the universal*, nothing but a (negative) element of universality as such, the particular as the (negative) element that expresses the universal. *The social is therefore not the fate or destiny of particularities. It is nevertheless a certain 'toward-which,' a 'that-toward-which' that is neither telos nor destination; perhaps, however, a lure Sociality can then only be thought, perversely, as the direction (and never the destination) of a certain movement, a certain precipitation, a 'that-toward-which' a certain curiosity . . ., a certain 'interested intuition' moves* (pp. 188–19, our emphasis)

Haver writes, then, that society is a 'necessarily impossible object' – in a constant state of reproduction, at once existing but always incomplete and in search of a way of reproducing itself: 'This implies that a certain essential incompletion or unaccomplishment is sociality itself: sociality is the impossibility of accomplishing an authentic identity present to itself, the impossibility of grounding truth in the Truth' (p. 191).

What we hope to gain from reading these dense passages is a sense of the ungraspability of the social – a sense of its fluidity – but also a glimpse of the presence of the erotic *as* sociality. We need to spend a little more time on that aspect of the social here, especially as the presence or absence of the erotic in arguments around sexual citizenship will be a common thread in some of our subsequent discussions.

It is precisely the explicitly sexual nature of some versions of queer theory (and practice) that critics such as Rosemary Hennessy find troubling. She writes that 'for lesbian and gay avant-garde theory, resistance is constructed as a matter of claiming an eroticized, desiring, ambivalent identity as queer' (Hennessy, 1993, p. 971) – that troubling 'moment of transgression' again. Sexuality as erotic play is here seen as *anti-social*, as against the social, yet for sexual dissidents the erotic has been at the very core and definition of sociality, of creating a society based on sexual intimacy. It is precisely this 'eroticized, desiring, ambivalent identity' that creates the most trouble for social and cultural theory; it is sexuality as erotic play that the left finds troublesome, since it cannot accommodate such a politics of pleasure alongside the victimology of class injustice. In this context, gay men on the scene are dismissed as apolitical for their hedonism and for putting pleasure on a stage. This reflects the notion that recreational sex between men is *wasteful*, this time because it diverts attention and energy from the *productive* use of labour – building the revolutionary struggle. As Simon Edge (1995) discusses in his account of being an activist in the Socialist Workers' Party (SWP), the class-based revolutionary project cannot find a space for the articulation of homosexual identity, since for the SWP the gay commercial scene was seen as implicated in capitalism.

The distinctiveness of Haver's imagining of the social is the centrality he accords eroticism as the foundation of sociality and politicality. The formulation of a *queer social theory* (as opposed to a social theory of queers) must attend to the erotic because, as Haver says, is not eroticism the basis for all social relations?

> If sociality is a 'that-toward-which' that is a movement rather than a destination, if sociality is always 'actualized' or 'realized' in and as that very movement but never as a fully constituted object (that is

also to say, never the actualization or realization of a possibility, for the possibility only appears as the realization or actualization of the movement), then the movement of realizing or actualizing sociality is ... first and last erotic.   (1996, p. 189)

If eroticism is the foundation of sociality, then power – politicality – is likewise essentially bound up with erotic attachments; as Haver notes, '[p]oliticality, as the desire for an encounter with otherness, and therefore the possibility of any politics, whatsoever, is in its essence *erotic*' (p. 20). We should be clear that this does not imply a naive celebration of the erotic, but rather the articulation of power relations invested in eroticism and its suppression.

As we have already noted, the privatization of the erotic (in, for example, sex laws) must be read as a limitation on social citizenship; the granting of rights in this circumscribed way means for Diane Richardson (1998, p. 89) that 'lesbians and gay men, though granted certain rights of citizenship, are not a legitimate social constituency'; moreover, since the prime site of rights claims for social inclusion rests on access to welfare, she suggests that sexual minorities are profoundly socially excluded thanks to the heterosexualized foundations of the welfare state and social policy. Given the current political potency of the discourse of social exclusion, it is unsurprising (though not unproblematic) to see rights claims focused on gaining social inclusion as currently central to lesbian and gay politics. One element of social exclusion that we would like to consider here concerns the material articulation of exclusion in spatial terms.

Social space

Earlier in this chapter we focused on the discussion of the distinction between the politics of redistribution and the politics of representation. What we would now like to add to this is work on the politics of space, which clearly emphasizes the extent to which struggles over *the identity of place* are both real and symbolic. In order to trace a path beyond the impasse between the debates on the politics of recognition and redistribution – the social and the cultural – it may be helpful to consider the spatial. As we noted earlier in *The Sexual Citizen*, we consider space absolutely central to understanding how citizenship and rights claims operate. Sexual citizenship is locationally specific in all kinds of ways. Moreover, as we have already seen in our discussion of Bech's work, (homo-) sexual identity is the product of social space. If we can begin to think about how the social is constructed as a material and symbolic space, then we can perhaps begin to think about spatial strategies for sexual citizenship that might shift the meanings of the social itself.

In the conclusion to her examination of the transnationalization of citizenship, based on her study of the parameters of citizenship for Turkish migrants in Berlin, Yasemin Soysal (1994, p. 166) argues that membership of the community is based 'in a shared public, social space; a set of abstract principles and responsibilities; and the rationalized organization and routine of everyday praxis, independent of the specificities of the locale in which they live'. While Soysal does not address the politics of space explicitly, it is implicit in her argument that social space is fundamental to citizenship claims. There are clear parallels between her discussion of Turkish migrant citizenship and work on sexual citizenship – the formulation quoted above could equally have been lifted from *When Men Meet*. Clearly, citizenship is fundamentally materialized in space, for Turkish 'guest workers' as much as for sexual minorities.

Other writers have explored how struggles for citizenship claims are increasingly expressed in the assertion of spatial rights – in the right to occupy space. For instance, Davina Cooper's (1998) study of the politics of what she terms 'talmudic territory' demonstrates the extent to which space has become central to debates over difference, identity and rights claims. Cooper's discussion of the debates around the establishment of an eruv in Barnet, North London – a marked boundary that enables orthodox Jews to push and carry on the Sabbath by effectively making the space within the perimeter *private* space – shows that the struggle over the symbolic meaning of space is inseparable from the materiality of the built landscape, but that it is also a struggle for resources and power.

The eruv debates in Barnet demonstrate the extent to which public space in the UK is seen as naturalized as Christian, in the same way that space is normalized as heterosexual:

There are clearly parallels here with the opposition expressed towards public expressions of homosexuality. Heterosexual demonstrations are so naturalised they remain unapparent – wearing wedding/engagement rings, talking about marriage/honeymoons/dating, kissing/holding hands in public places. However, analogous signifiers of sexuality by lesbians and gay men, lacking a naturalised status, remain highly visible, and are construed as flaunting. (Cooper, 1998, p. 133).

In Barnet, objectors argued that the establishment of the eruv would mean one group (orthodox Jews) gaining spatial rights, and that this would lead to a slippery slope of all manner of 'special interest groups' demanding equal treatment and spatial rights under the law.

Cooper's study of talmudic territory shows us that space and boundaries are used to make distinctions between self and other; the enclosure of space is fundamental to distinctions between insiders and outsiders. Social exclusion is increasingly characterized by exclusion from space: 'in order to understand the problem of exclusion in modern society, we need a cultural reading of space' (Sibley, 1995, p. 72) – though our reading must recognize that space itself is not merely cultural. In this context the notion of urban life as the *democratic* encounter with difference – the place where strangers meet – is unsustainable, given the geographies of exclusion that overlay city-space (see chapter 5). What this means is that utopian formulations of sexual citizenship envisaged in accounts of sites for public sex and queer consumption must address questions of social and economic inequality as they map over those sites. It is not a simple question of an affirmation of shopping and fucking in a time of reaction and family values. For instance, the supposedly liberatory spaces of radical sexual democracy – bathhouses, for example – were (and indeed still are) in practice far from democratic and inclusive; African-American men, for example, were (are) routinely excluded from such spaces in US cities. Similarly, non-affluent gays were (are) excluded from the bathhouse culture by dint of their low incomes (see chapter 6). The changing economic geography of public sex means that cruising areas are one of the few social spaces that exist outside of the market – however, the gendered nature of the public/private divide is reflected in the few spaces for public sex for women, adding a further dimension to spatialized social exclusion.

In this chapter, we have examined some quite different imaginings of the social, thinking through the ways that capitalism reacts or relates to homosexuality, exploring ways of seeing a distinct homosexual form of the social, and calling for the inclusion of sexuality as erotic play in theories of sociality. We have argued that struggles over real and symbolic space may be useful in progressing the discussion beyond a simple dichotomy of redistribution versus recognition, and that we need to see social exclusion as manifest in space. In the next chapter, we shall be exploring a particular mode of sociality-in-space: that to be found in the city.

5

Sexual Democracy and Urban Life

As we stated at the start of *The Sexual Citizen*, we have a particular interest in thinking about spaces of sexual citizenship. In the previous chapter we examined a number of different framings of the social, which ended by focusing on social space. Arguably the most relevant stage for thinking about the social nature of sexuality is the city. The city is the prime site both for the materialization of sexual identity, community and politics, and for conflicts and struggles around sexual identity, community and politics, and in this chapter we want to address specifically the urban basis of sexual citizenship. Any discussion of sexual citizenship must examine the city: how cities work, and who they work for. We will argue that we must have a much more critical understanding of the city itself. *Cities are different from one another, and in their treatment of sexual diversity*; this notion permits us to elaborate a clearer focus on the city, and we will use the concept to focus our discussion on how and why sexual citizenship is constructed differently in different cities.

The treatment of the city as sexualized space provided by Henning Bech in *When Men Meet* (1997) represents easily the most imaginative study of the urban basis of gay male citizenship. Bech argues that the city is *the* home of the homosexual:

In the city, the homosexual makes contact. It is usually established by means of glance and signals – or in instances where glance cannot be used, by touching or listening. It is possible of course to meet strangers anywhere – at work, at friends' and acquaintances' – but the city is *the* proper place for that kind of meeting, and there are also special places here particularly well-suited or even tailored to the purpose.   (p. 110)

For Bech, the city *enables* sexualities to be materialized. Specifically, it is the desire of a man for another man that Bech is concerned with. For men having sex with other men, the city is a stage where lust is generated:

> the city is not merely a stage on which a pre-existing, preconstructed sexuality is displayed and acted out; it is also a space where sexuality is generated. What is it about the city that stimulates? Surely that altogether special blend of closeness and distance, crowd and flickering, surface and gaze, freedom and danger. Others are defenceless vis-à-vis your gaze and you yourself are on display to theirs; you come so close to them that you can actually touch them, yet ought not to: a distance that incites you to overstep yet still maintain it; surfaces intercept gazes and turn into signals, and the flickering vibrates; the crowd generates feelings of supply and possibilities; the anonymity and the absence of immediate social control amplifies the feeling, and the risk of nevertheless being monitored and uncovered increases the tension. You sense this omnipresent, diffuse sexualization of the city and confirm it by designing your surface accordingly and by taking up a position, perhaps also by engaging in cruising and brief encounters.   (p. 118)

Bech argues that there is something essentially *democratic* in these encounters with strangers, in a similar vein to writers such as Edmund White writing about the democracy of the bathhouse in his *States of Desire* (1980) – in fact, Dianne Chisholm (1999, p. 71) reads the gay bathhouse as a *concentration* of the city, 'incorporating big-city lights in a perverse totalization of urban space'. While we wish to embrace this ideal utopian vision of queer urbanity, the reality is far more complex. The production of queer spaces and citizenship means *inclusion* for some, but also implies the *exclusion* of others: not all queers are equally free to gain from these encounters. *Where* the encounters take place is essential to our reading of their democratic potential. For example, spaces that are bounded or closed (commercial territories such as bathhouses) may restrict entrance and exclude on, for example, economic or discriminatory grounds. Mobility is increasingly the pre-requisite for participation in these spaces – many bathhouses are located not in the centre of the city, but rather in suburban areas, on industrial estates or in outlying commuter towns. Gay bars are similarly not without boundaries, dress codes, rules; they also operate systems of inclusion and exclusion. Belonging is therefore dependent on one's resources (or resourcefulness). Writing about his own experiences as a gay man moving to San Francisco, Allan Bérubé (1996, p. 152) reflects on the exclusionary economic geography of the city's gay commercial and residential spaces: 'What I experienced most directly as a white gay man with little money and no college degree was how the gay community reproduced class hierarchies. There were many gay restaurants, disco parties, conferences, resorts, and bathhouses I couldn't afford. And I didn't have the income to live in the Castro.'

Poverty not only promotes homophobia; it also denies the 'enabling resources' of sexual citizenship to working-class lesbians and gay men. Poverty means that spatial solutions to resolving the conflicts associated with a queer identity and the particular localized experience of homophobia in place (solutions such as permanent or temporary migration, or holidays to 'gay resorts' and global gay cities) are denied because poverty puts a brake on mobility. This is important because spatial solutions to the management of gay identity are treated simplistically by some authors, as if these consumption practices are open to all. As we have seen from Bérubé's memoirs, even those cities that have been at the heart of the 'great gay migration' fail to live up to their promise for many who move there but lack the resources to live metropolitan gay life. Similarly, the discussions of gay men as urban pioneers in the gentrification process (such as Knopp, 1995) overlook the housing problems faced by less economically mobile gay city residents, whose spatial mobility is often forced rather than a 'lifestyle decision'.

Moreover, there is an economic geography to public space which impacts profoundly on non-commercial queer sites. Commenting on the new zoning laws in New York City targeted at sex shops and porn cinemas, Lauren Berlant and Michael Warner (1998) note that the queerness of the streets is fragile and can never be taken for granted. They also point to the economic basis of queer urban space:

> Because the heteronormative culture of intimacy leaves queer cul-
> ture especially dependent on ephemeral elaborations in urban
> space...queer publics are also peculiarly vulnerable to initiatives
> such as Mayor Randolph Giuliani's new zoning law. The law aims to
> restrict any counterpublic sexual culture by regulating its economic
> conditions; its effects will reach far beyond the adult businesses
> it explicitly controls. The gay bars on Christopher Street draw cus-
> tomers from people who come there because of its sex trade. The
> street is cruisier because of the sex shops.   (p. 562)

So, the city's economically led (but also homophobically motivated) rezoning also closes down sites of 'counterpublic sexual culture'. Public spaces such as streets have long been central to (particularly gay male) sexual citizenship, especially for those marginalized by class or race (Chauncey, 1996; Leap, 1999). Accounts of gay uses of streets tend to stress the democratic nature of activities such as cruising – as we have seen from Bech, the gay man is a kind of sexualized *flâneur*, relishing the opportunities to gaze and cruise. However, we need to think more carefully about the workings of the gaze in the city, and recognize the presence of the homophobic gaze alongside the homosexual gaze. This brings us on to questions of who gazes on whom in the fleeting play of strangers that is the city.

Looking at sameness and difference

Bech sees the city as the stage for gay men to become visible to one another – in one sense a desire for *sameness*, for those who are like oneself; hence the pull of cities for dissident sexual citizens (Weston, 1995). Elsewhere, however, the dominant take on urban desire tends to restate and reproduce a straight gaze looking – and what it is looking for is *difference*. Iris Marion Young's (1990) discussion of the latent eroticism in urban living, for example, denotes a different kind of erotics. For Young the eroticism of city life lies within the romantic consumption of *difference*:

City life also instantiates difference as the erotic, in the wide sense of an attraction to the other, the pleasure and excitement of being drawn out of one's secure routine to encounter the novel, strange, and surprising. The erotic dimension of the city has always been an aspect of its fearfulness, for it holds out the possibility that one will lose one's identify, will fall.   (p. 239)

Presumably lesbians and gay men – as exotic others – are one group that Young would see as a novel minority to be experienced, colonized and consumed in a similar manner to ethnic groups:

> But we also take pleasure in being open to and interested in people we experience as different. We spend a Sunday afternoon walking through Chinatown, or checking out this week's eccentric players in the park. We look for restaurants, stores, and clubs with something new for us, a new ethnic food, a different atmosphere, a different crowd of people. We walk through sections of the city that we experience as having unique characters which are not ours, where people from diverse places mingle and then go home.   (p. 239)

Young goes on to argue that the erotic attraction she discusses is 'precisely the obverse of community. In the ideal of community people feel affirmed because those with whom they share experiences, perceptions, and goals recognize and are recognized by them; one sees oneself reflected in the others' (p. 239). But queer identity comes into being through these encounters with strangers. It is precisely through these encounters on the street with other queers that one forms one's sense of community, of belonging (Bell and Binnie, 1998). For Young it is the encounter with the unfamiliar – losing rather than finding one's sense of self – that is exciting, and in her eyes erotic.

Eroticism for Young, then, is counterposed against community; yet for queers *eroticism is the basis of community*. As Sally Munt (1995) writes, her encounters with the similar – other lesbians in butch drag – bring with them the intelligibility of the familiar and the attractive that constitutes and affirms her very sense of self and of home: 'Briefly returning to Brighton for the summer, my eye follows a woman wearing a wide-shouldered linen suit. Down the street, she starts to decelerate. I zip up my jacket, put my best foot forward, and tell myself that "home" is just around the corner'

(p. 125). When Young writes about going home, she means that place where her identity is secure and solid – in the private sphere. For Munt (and other queers), 'home' of course means something completely different.

So, albeit in very different ways, we have seen that both Bech and Young mythologize and romanticize the city. Their writings on the city tend to asssume a cosmopolitan city and a cosmopolitan vision of urban life (Binnie and Skeggs, 1999), when in fact cities are far more diverse than their accounts give credit for – we simply cannot agree with Bech's assertion in a later essay that '*urban sexualization* constitutes a modern *universal*, running counter to the accentuation of the local and the particular, a *homogenizing* complication for the celebration of difference' (1999, p. 228). In the next section, *contra* Bech, we will examine how and why cities differ in their sexing of space. We also note that cities are plural, not singular – we need to be sensitive to the multiplicity of cities experienced as London, for example. Microgeographies of sexual citizenship do matter – as Young herself puts it, the city is 'a place of many places' (1990, p. 240).

A place of many places

While Bech's perspective on the city is fabulous, it is nevertheless somewhat utopian and exclusionary – for one thing, his discussion of the city as the place where men meet is predicated on the exclusion of women from the city (or at least from Bech's discussion of it). A more fundamental problem we find with both Bech's and Young's perspectives is the implied *homogeneity* of 'the city'. It is hard to recognize many cities in the descriptions both writers provide us with. Some cities, rather than being nurturing of difference, are notoriously resistant to it. It should be a pretty obvious (but nevertheless slightly boring) geographical observation that cities are different from one another. Their openness to sexual citizens is itself a barometer of a city's openness towards difference and diversity.

What this means is that we need to be more attuned to which types of city more or less share the qualities outlined by Young and Bech. Moreover, we should begin to understand how and why cities change *vis-à-vis* their treatment of difference and in their attitudes towards the development of queer space within their borders. One of the surprising features of the urban sexual geography of the UK in the late 1990s, for instance, is the development of queer commercial spaces within two cities hitherto noted for their underdeveloped gay scenes and their resistance to queerness – Glasgow and Birmingham. We would argue that a political-economic analysis is necessary here, given the fact that these changes do not take place in a vacuum. The centres of these cities underwent dramatic changes in the mid-1990s, with Glasgow City Council's controversial and contested policy of promoting economic regeneration through support of art and cultural projects in the city, and Birmingham's bid to become a major European city through its support for the International Convention Centre, which has raised the international profile of the city as it plays host to major international events such as the G-8 Summit and the Eurovision Song Contest. Cities, then, vary over time – and this can be both positive and negative in terms of their orientation to spaces of dissident sexual citizenship, as the transformations of Glasgow and Birmingham are an outcome of the same pressures that have led to New York's new zoning laws.

A recognition of the differences between and within cities has immediate consequences for how we conceive of urban space; we need to displace the reductionism in Young and Bech, where the city is represented as a single entity or concept. (This line of thinking, widely reflected in writing on urban theory, is classed by Nigel Thrift (2000) as a prominent 'urban myth': that 'one city tells all'.) Running parallel to Gayle Rubin's (1993) hierarchy of dangerous sexualities, we need an urban hierarchy of desires – a map of what is possible in particular cities and parts of cities: we must be more attuned to the local and the particular when we talk about the city. For example, Manchester and Sheffield are both large postindustrial cities in the north of England, but they vary tremendously in terms of the visibility of sexual cultures and the performative urban sexual citizenship outlined above (Taylor, Evans and Fraser, 1996). In discussing the urban basis of sexual citizenship, what we need more than anything else, then, is a sense of perspective. In this regard we share Doreen Massey's concern that the focus in urban theory on major cities such as Los Angeles and New York, Paris and

London obscures 'the relative unimportance of these places, in quantitative terms, in the context of world-wide twenty-first-century city life' (1995, p. 100).

Not all cities are equally enabling or facilitating of particular identities, then. In fact, regional or provincial cities have often been conceptualized within queer culture as uniformly oppressive places, set against global 'gay meccas' such as San Francisco. Regional cities are commonly represented as, in the words of the Pet Shop Boys, 'the place I waited years to leave'. Yet recently a number of regional cities (such as Manchester and Antwerp) have gained in status and reputation as gay-friendly, and have established themselves as destinations on the international gay tourist market. We should also note here Davina Cooper's (1994) work on 'the activist state' in regional British cities, which demonstrates a highly uneven pattern of involvement in urban sexual politics, mapping a complex micropolitical geography of activism: 'Even within Britain's major cities, lesbian and gay policy development was very uneven, and largely absent in the sizeable conurbations of Leeds, Birmingham and Sheffield. Why a progressive sexual politics developed in some areas but not others is an interesting question that requires further research' (p. 114).

Sally Munt's (1995) essay on the lesbian *flâneur* vividly demonstrates the different experiences of ownership of the city's streets in different British regional urban centres. She narrates her own experiences in Brighton and Nottingham, writing that '[a] four-hour drive separates the two, but in terms of my lesbian identity, I'm in another country' (p. 114). As part of the answer to the question that Cooper raises about the uneven development of urban sexual politics, Munt is quick to point to the heavy manufacturing tradition of Nottingham as one explanation for what she perceives as the particularly oppressive experience of being a lesbian in that city. Possession of the city's streets, one's comfort in asserting one's sexual identity in public space, is a marker of sexual citizenship, then, for Munt – and she enjoys only a restricted sexual citizenship in Nottingham:

> There's nothing like being contained in its two large shopping malls on a Saturday morning to make one feel queer. Inside again, this pseudo-public space is sexualised as privately heterosexual. Displays

of intimacy over the purchase of family sized commodities are exchanges of gazes calculated to exclude. When the gaze turns, its intent is hostile: visual and verbal harassment make me avert my eyes. (p. 115)

As we signalled earlier, Munt's description of being queer in Nottingham reminds us of the presence of the homophobic gaze; moreover, her discussion of the experience of Brighton and Nottingham reinforces our point about different cities being different places for dissident sexual citizens. In order to illustrate this point further, we want to mention a recent British legal case – the trial of the so-called 'Bolton 7' (see also Binnie, 2000). Bolton is a large, predominantly working-class town in the northwest of England, only twenty minutes by road or rail from Manchester. In 1997 seven men from Bolton were arrested and subsequently prosecuted for consensual same-sex activities in their homes – or, as the law would see them, for serious imprisonable sexual offences occurring in public (Moran, 1999). One notable aspect of the trial was that the working-class backgrounds and local identities of the defendants were mobilized against them, marking them as 'unsophisticated' (especially since they did not even know that the acts they engaged in were illegal). As Les Moran notes, in the context of a case like that of the 'Bolton 7', 'it is important to take parochialism seriously in order to understand the specificity of space and place' (p. 40). The men's 'provincial' status, especially in relation to nearby metropolitan Manchester's well-developed gay scene, reveals the uneven development of sexual citizenship in space.

This uneven development is still more remarkably evident in contrasting urban and rural locations. Work on the lived experiences of lesbians and gay men in rural areas frequently focuses on isolation and a chronic lack of the resources for queer sexual citizenship that are taken for granted in cities (Bell, 2000; Kramer, 1995). Moreover, as the rural men interviewed by Will Fellows in *Farm Boys* (1996) often said, homosexuality tends to be seen by country folk as an urban phenomenon irrelevant to rural living. The stresses of rural gay life, therefore, have often resulted in migration to cities, which are constructed in the gay imaginary as 'beacons of tolerance and gay community', in contrast to the country's construction as 'a locus of persecution and gay absence' (Weston, 1995, p. 282).

This should remind us that we have also to consider relations between places – Bolton and Manchester, the country and the city. Moreover, we need to understand the *relations between cities* in forming transnational cultural space (see chapter 7). When it comes to queerness, we need not only to articulate the position of London, New York and Los Angeles within queer culture, but also to locate them within the connections made by the global economy, since new economic forces shape and reshape the production of dissident sexual spaces. So, when we turn our attention to the global city, we must be aware that even in this context (perhaps, in fact, *particularly* in this context) one city similarly hides a multitude of different experiences for sexual dissidents.

The global queer city

Global cities play an important role in queer signification, as places to escape to; but, as Massey (1995) has warned us, not all global cities are the same – and not all global cities have a queer resonance; they are differently sexualized. Singapore, for example, is a highly restrictive society in which any form of permissiveness is clamped down on. The particular state ideology of the family within Singaporean society means that sexual dissidence is surpressed, so urban space is differently sexualized there.

For queers on a global scale, particular cities have clear resonances, often within a utopian imagined geography. New York, for example, has a particular symbolic (even mythical) function, linked to Stonewall and thereby to the birth of the lesbian and gay rights movement (see Seidman, 1998). Sally Munt (1995, p. 125) speaks of the fabulousness associated with New York City as a global queer capital, writing that 'For lesbian and gay people it has a particular set of meanings and associations, and so to resist mythologising New York is a difficult practice to perform.' There are links at work here between cities, bringing back into play the issue of the spatial solutions to place-specific homophobia we mentioned earlier. Lauren Berlant and Michael Warner argue that the zoning laws in New York aim to reinforce the idea of a stable community based on property ownership and residence:

The ideology of the neighborhood is politically unchallengeable in the current debate, which is dominated by a fantasy that sexual subjects only reside, that the space relevant to sexual politics is the neighborhood. But a district like Christopher Street is not just a neighborhood affair. The local character of the neighborhood depends on the daily presence of thousands of nonresidents. Those who actually live in the West Village should not forget their debt to these mostly queer pilgrims. *And we should not make the mistake of confusing the class of citizens with the class of property owners. Many of those who hang out on Christopher Street – typically young, queer, and African American – couldn't possibly afford to live there. Urban space is always a host space. The right to the city extends to those who use the city. It is not limited to property owners.* (1998, p. 563, our emphasis)

Thus local legislation has consequences well beyond the borders of the neighbourhood, since Christopher Street has a symbolic meaning worldwide (reflected, for example, in pride marches in German cities being called 'Christopher Street Days'). Martin Manalansan IV notes that this is equally clear in the globalization of the myth of Stonewall. Recalling the official guide to the twenty-fifth anniversary celebrations of the Stonewall riot, he argues that 'the textualization of Stonewall has changed – from localized descriptions of a police raid on a Greenwich Village bar to globalized descriptions of a revolutionary moment for gays and lesbians everywhere' (Manalansan, 1995, p. 427). While New York enjoys mythic status worldwide, other cities may have quite different resonances. For first world queers, cities like Manilla and Bangkok have a distinct appeal, bringing to our attention a complex ethical and moral question emerging out of globalization. Moves by the UK government to follow Sweden's example and make it a crime for a national to partake in sex with minors outside of the borders of one's own state will clearly rewrite the sexual geographies of these particular global cities.

Global queer cities play a major symbolic role in queer identification (as long as we remember the cautions we have already signalled). Whether you have never visited New York, Los Angeles, Sydney, Amsterdam or Berlin is less relevant than the fact that you dream about visiting them one day – or at least that you know that they are there. They have thus become important sites of queer pilgrimage, especially for affluent gay international tourists.

Accounts of gay tourism, however, tend to overlook the power-geometry of the spatialities of this flow of people. It is assumed that the queer tourist is a free agent who can move openly in global society – yet this itself must not be overstated, for the rights he or she will enjoy vary considerably from one nation-state to the next. The movements of gay tourists around the world trace complex maps of both myth and materiality, of possibility and constraint, of freedom and oppression. A full cartography of these movements has yet to be drawn. Moreover, as we show in chapter 7, we must also remember other flows of people across transnational space – exiles, refugees and immigrants (Appadurai, 1996) – who move for different motives, and experience mobility in profoundly different ways. The global city, perhaps most of all, is a place of many places; it is also a place of many people – who build many different life-spaces, relationships and communities in urban space.

Cities as networks of love and friendship

We need to think about the kinds of relationship that are brought together in the city – if the city brings us into citizenship-relations with others, which kind of citizenship-relations are the most important? It is a helpful first step towards answering this question to consider the kinds of queer space that are materialized in the city: is the queer city a space of residence, or of commerce? A space of friendship, of community? An erotic space? Of course, cities are all of these – but the extent of the development of different kinds of space is context-specific to particular cities. Histories of particular cities show the ways in which these queer spaces develop and change over time, and often point to an increasing 'institutional thickness' and diversification (Higgs, 1999). Some cities – Manchester is a good example – have undergone an incredible period of development and 'thickening', with its 'gay village' moving from a position of a few scruffy bars a decade ago to today's thriving commercial scene with over fifty gay-related businesses, substantial residential developments and a key role to play in the city's place-promotion strategies (Binnie and Skeggs, 1999).

Of course, this has not been without cost, especially in terms of marginalizing other kinds of sexual space – especially those of sex work and public sex. In a number of important recent interventions in queer theory, it is precisely these spaces that are signalled as offering the most radical and utopian possibilities for a new modality of dissident sexual citizenship. They are also the most fragile and embattled: it should be clear by now that these spaces of intimate citizenship are transitory, and themselves prone to the workings of the urban land economy and the forces of global capital. It is a paradox in many major cities that the increased visibility of sexual dissidents in the commercial heartland has served to reinforce the marginalization of public sex (Binnie, 2000). For example, San Francisco's push for global city status has consequences in the economic restructuring of the commercial leathersex zones in the SOMA district (Rubin, 1998); similar processes are at work in New York and in Amsterdam (Binnie, 1995; Duyves, 1995).

The cleaning-up of the sex zone goes hand in hand with an ideology of the production of safe domestic space, where families can occupy space without the threat of contagion from alternative forms of intimacy. It is a further paradox, of course, that gay cultural producers are often complicit in this process. So, while queer writers urge a widening of the zone of intimacy, these laboratories of sex, love and friendship are being forced out of the urban built environment, with profound impacts for the cultures of sexual citizenship in all our cities. In their place, as we have seen, are capital-sanctioned spaces for sexual citizenship – commercial scenes, gentrified neighbourhoods and the like. In the next chapter, we shall explore the ways in which the myth of gay consumerism has impacted upon formulations of sexual citizenship, through a discussion of the pink economy.

6

The Love that Dares Not
Forget its Brand Name

The title for this chapter comes from an article on lesbian and gay business (also known as the pink economy) that appeared in the UK's *Financial Times* newspaper (Gould, 1998). Commenting on the growth of lesbian and gay venues in the West End of London, Paul Gould restates familiar discourses on the pink economy imported from the USA. Rather dubious evidence is put forward for the growth in what he terms 'the gradual acceptance of homosexuals', such as the fact that 'Waterstone's bookstores have lesbian and gay sections; Virgin's megastore on Oxford Street stocks gay videos; [and] the BBC's long-running soap *EastEnders* has introduced a gay couple to Albert Square'. Gould states that gays constitute what he terms a 'marketing man's dream', and uncritically quotes proponents of the pink economic miracle, such as Liz Mackenzie, who claims that 'all new dance, fashion and club music trends seem to spring from the gay market' (p. xxii). In this chapter we want to interrogate some of these myths critically, and to move towards providing a more nuanced account of the many economic aspects of sexual citizenship.

In his essay 'The political economy of the closet' (1997), Jeffrey Escoffier has suggested that the current phase of the development of lesbian and gay communities is one characterized by 'hyper-commodification, as mainstream corporations target the homo/market niche with consumer goods and advertising' (p. 124). We shall argue here that the power that queer citizens enjoy is largely dependent on access to capital and credit: global capitalism shapes our very existence. The discourse of the pink economy constructs queers as model consumer-citizens and therefore as builders of stable communities. Happy gay couples – the perfect DINKs (Dual Income No Kids) – are said to make a disproportionate economic contribution to society. Here we want to subject the myth of the pink economy to close scrutiny. We argue that any discussion of the economic position and status of lesbians and gay men must acknowledge: (1) the potential for homophobia within representations of gay men and lesbians as an affluent group in society; (2) the invisibility of discussions of homophobia within these representations; (3) the class and other differences between lesbians, gay men and other sexual dissidents, which directly impact on the extent of their participation in the pink economy.

The glamour and hype of the pink economy

At the start of the twenty-first century one could be forgiven for thinking that lesbians and gay men are economic angels, blessing the economy with miracles of unlimited spending. It has now become a commonplace assumption that lesbians, and more notably gay men, are model consumers, miracle workers in the new urban service economy of postindustrial, post-Fordist western society. One indication of the extent of this view is its parody by M.V. Lee Badget:

> It doesn't look like a bad life. You graduate from college, attend a prestigious business school, and land a first job offering a compensation package worth close to $100,000. You move up the ranks in a financially and intellectually satisfying career. You develop networks of diverse and powerful friends and colleagues. You travel the world with your cosmopolitan friends. Companies with products to sell actively seek your business and fear your anger. Society sees you as creative, a fashion trendsetter. Your employer tries to create a work environment that allows you to maximize your productive capabilities. Unfortunately, this is not a life that one can simply choose but one that depends on the luck of birth. The victors of this genetic draw are those who are fortunate enough to be born lesbian or gay. (1997b, pp. 607–8)

Lee Badget lampoons the view that lesbians and gay men occupy a privileged status *vis-à-vis* the market economy. As she hints, such views tend to downplay homophobia in the workplace and emphasize an assimilationist politics of identity based on essentialism – that lesbian and gay workers can be 'good-as-you'. African-American and Latino writers have long challenged the ethnocentricity of these assumptions, and asserted the significance of differential access to the enabling resources of citizenship for black queers as well as the invisibility of black queers in the discourses of the model gay citizen, who is constructed as middle-class, suburban and white. Barbara Smith contests a number of dangerous notions that can give rise to homophobic sentiment:

> 'Gay' means gay white men with large discretionary incomes, period. Perceiving gay people in this way allows one to ignore that some of us are women *and* people of color *and* working class *and* poor *and* disabled *and* old. Thinking narrowly of gay people as white, middle class, and male, which is just what the establishment media want people to think, undermines consciousness of how identities and issues overlap.   (1993, p. 101)

While Smith's statement gestures towards a history of the awareness of the links between class, capital and sexuality, it is only very recently that systematic work has been carried out on the economic basis of sexual dissidence (though see earlier work by D'Emilio (1993) and Rubin (1993)). More recently, work has appeared from economists arguing that the pink economy is little more than a myth. A number of contributors to the edited volume *Homo Economics* (Gluckman and Reed, 1997) make important interventions into the emerging debate on the political economy of sexuality. In her essay 'Beyond biased samples', for example, Lee Badget dissects some of the misleading statistics that are often banded about in discussions of the economic muscle of the USA's lesbian and gay population:

> Some gay and lesbian people are wealthy and, therefore, are particularly attractive targets for advertising, just as some heterosexual people are wealthy and are highly sought after by many marketers. But some gay and lesbian people are poor, and most are somewhere in the middle along with the majority of heterosexual people. As the

best available academic studies show, the real economic difference comes from the harmful effects of employment discrimination against lesbian, gay and bisexual people. Those studies confirm what other groups facing discrimination also know: discrimination doesn't just hurt psychologically – it hits people in their pocketbooks.   (1997a, p. 70)

In chapter 4 we argued that the framing of struggles around sexuality as 'merely cultural' masks the real economic situation of poverty and discrimination that affects lesbians and gay men on a daily basis. This raises a fundamental question: Is there a distinct relationship that lesbians and gay men occupy as a group within the economic system, or should the stress be rather on the differences between lesbians and gay men on the basis of class, race and disability? Some writers hold the latter view. For example, in an interview, Barbara Smith (1997) argues that lesbian and gay oppression is not economically determined. She goes on to argue that lesbians and gay men as a group do not have a particular relationship to capitalism, but rather that class differences are more salient:

> As with all groups, I think that our economic system has the most implications for lesbians and gay men when their class position makes them vulnerable to that economic system. So in other words, it's not that in general being lesbian and gay puts you into a critical relationship to capitalism, it's that a large proportion of lesbians and gay men are poor and working class, but of course they're completely invisible the way the movement's politics are defined now.   (p. 196)

This statement reminds us of the arguments around queer politics – that the focus on the 'lifestylization' of sexual politics in queer has invisibilized class difference (Fraser, 1999). In an era of lifestyle politics, then, queer politics becomes just one more brand name to buy into (Evans, 1993). Moreover, Smith suggests that the mainstreaming and respectability of 'gay specific issues' in the assimilationist agenda also masks conflicts around racism and socioeconomic inequalities, since the arguments always seem to depend on a 'model gay citizen' who is white and middle-class. In this context, she is particularly hostile towards domestic partnerships:

> Domestic partnership is about looking at the society the way we know it and saying: 'I want some of that, it's not fair that I don't have it. I want access to my partner's health insurance policy.' Of course, this assumes that partner *has* health insurance. It's a way of getting the benefits that certain people get under this system. As long as we live under this system, all people should have access to the same benefits regardless of sexual orientation.   (1997, p. 201)

One conclusion that should be drawn from our discussion of this important intervention into the debate is that gay men must not be stereotyped as uniformly affluent, nor should lesbians be represented as uniformly poor. Sexuality is cross-cut by class, race and gender in complex ways, which the prevailing myths of the affluent gay consumer in the pink economy invisibilize.

It is thus important to make explicit the homophobic nature of the pink economy discourse. Evans (1993) and others, for example, make simplistic links between the 'inversion' of gender in queer identities and the consumption patterns of sexual dissidents (gay men shop, lesbians don't). Moreover, among many commentators on queer consumption there is a tendency either to demonize and pathologize gay men as shallow, passive consumers – as both victims of and exploiters of capitalism – or conversely to celebrate the creative, radical and innovative nature of gay consumer culture. Both discourses can too easily assume a homophobic tone, but do so in differently offensive manners.

Part of the problem in addressing the pink economy comes from the left's critical stance on consumption *per se*. In *Over the Rainbow*, Nicola Field (1995, p. 175) argues that 'of all the groups of people ranged in opposition to injustice, inequality and oppression, it is workers who are the most organized and the most potentially powerful'. For Field the only answer is class struggle, and all paths point towards the Socialist Workers' Party (SWP). Field's solutions to the class-based nature of homophobic oppression, however, fail to take into account the experiences of others in the SWP who point to widespread homophobia within the organization itself (Edge, 1995). Once again, the problematic relationship between the left and sexual politics is brought into sharp relief. As we noted in chapter 4, Guy Hocquenghem theorized the connection between capitalism and homosexuality in *Homosexual Desire*, arguing that 'the anti-capitalist movement can often be pro-family, and indeed anti-homosexual' (1993, p. 93). His study was first published in French in 1972, which demonstrates that resistance to homophobia on the left has a long history. In *With Friends Like These* (1995), Simon Edge, a gay man and former SWP activist, argues that his fellow SWP activists discouraged him from going out on the gay scene because it was supposedly an exploitative manifestation of the capitalist mode of production. After trying desperately hard to be a good Marxist by avoiding the evils of the scene, Edge finally succumbed to temptation, came out on the scene, developed a gay identity and then unsurprisingly (perhaps) left the SWP:

> After a relatively small number of years, I ventured into the place that dare not speak its name (in the SWP, at any rate) and discovered what I would have found long before had I not been so plain stupid: that, for someone who has spent their entire life surrounded by heterosexuals and heterosexuality, the social and sexual economy of other gay people is profoundly liberating.   (p. 12)

Edge writes that in the SWP any assertion of an independent gay identity was deemed to be suspect, as this detracted from the collective project of class struggle. SWP activists argued that class struggle and the fight against homophobia were inextricably linked. Therefore, according to this logic, to commit yourself to class war meant that you could not be homophobic. However, Edge recounts the SWP's failure to address gay political issues as valid issues in their own right, but only when they were seen as relevant to their own political causes.

Edge's experiences reflect the considerable ignorance on the straight left of the everyday lives of lesbians and gay men. There is a nasty history of homophobia and heterosexism on the left that must be acknowledged; Andrew Parker (1993, p. 21) argues that this is linked to the left's suspicion of sex and pleasure: 'why has thinking sex proven to be so difficult for Western Marxism? Why, if never simply or entirely an absence, does sexuality form an *aporia*, a blockage within the tradition's production-centered paradigm?' He notes that when sex and sexuality are mentioned by Marxist writers, they see them only as things that have come to be colonized by capital.

Writing in 1994, Derek Cohen (a former member of the Gay Left collective) expressed his bemusement that, while the struggle for socialism was now looking rather forlorn, the struggle for gay liberation appeared to be in an altogether healthier state. In a statement perhaps calculated to raise the hackles of the (gay) left, Cohen argues that gay liberation 'has been furthered as much by consumer spending as by demonstrations', adding that capitalism 'can as easily deliver gay liberation as Gucci loafers' (quoted in Edge, 1995, p. 14). This pro-market argument has been used in sexual politics to argue that consumption can be mobilized politically – a position untenable to the traditional left's continued staining of shopping with the logic of commodity fetishism. This logic has, furthermore, come to stain gay consumers as commodity fetishists *par excellence*:

> Recently, a new stereotype has crept into the antihomosexual literature of the right. In addition to being portrayed as immoral, disease-ridden child molesters, gay men and lesbians are now described as superwealthy, highly-educated free spenders. The economic arguments that have begun to appear in the past few years are an important part of the same strategy: to split the gay community off from what might have appeared to be its natural allies in a broad, progressive civil-rights movement. (Hardisty and Gluckman, 1997, p. 218)

This tension, neatly summed up by Rosaria Champagne (1998, p. 282) as the risk of 'turning queer theory [and politics] into commodity queerness', continues to emphasize the troubling alignment of sexual politics and consumer citizenship. While particular progressive political projects are enabled through the strategic use of the market – such as consumer boycotts of companies with homophobic practices – the broader articulation of rights claims via the market neglects the material circumstances that make such a politics possible (or impossible) in the first place. Nowhere is this tension more apparent than in debates around the economic impacts of the politics of visibility – politics that have long been central to sexual rights agitations.

The economic geography of the closet

> The visible existence of gay and lesbian communities is an important bulwark against the tide of reaction; the economic vitality of contemporary lesbian and gay communities erodes the ability of conservatives to reconstruct the closet. The closet is the specter that haunts lesbian and gay politics – and lurks in every social and political action that seeks to isolate and contain lesbian and gay communities. (Escoffier, 1997, p. 131)

It is a touchstone of radical gay politics that the closet is the framing device that scars lesbian and gay lives. As such, the politics of visibility encapsulated in coming out has long been seen as vital to claiming sexual rights. However, the economic costs of coming out are still present and important. In his essay on the economic history of the closet, Escoffier argues that the closet leads towards the spatial separation of everyday life: for example, in terms of work and leisure activities. Geographers of sexuality such as Gill Valentine (1993) have also argued that the spatial separation of activities is a major constraining feature of the lives of the lesbians she interviewed in her study, conducted in the English Home Counties in the early 1990s. This itself carries an economic burden – what Escoffier calls the 'transaction costs' of such a compartmentalized life. Further, the imperative to come out across all parts of everyday life (to friends, to family, at work) can also have profound economic impacts: for example in career choice, promotion prospects and relocation. The 'great gay migration' to the big cities, which hold the promise of realizing the dream of 'gay life', is itself attainable only at a price (Weston, 1995). Once there, finding somewhere to live, and somewhere to work, needn't necessarily be a liberation. And, of course, coming out – or being outed – can still get you sacked, as the hit movie *Philadelphia* vividly if problematically made clear (Holliday, 1998). Coming out, then, is a political move heavily marked by socioeconomic status and relative dependency within the economic system – this inevitably frames coming out and the different experiences of closetedness across the spatial-economic contexts of queer citizenship (see also Seidman, 1998). As Judith Butler (1993, p. 227) puts it, it is imperative that we ask for whom being out is 'a historically available and affordable option' before it is declared a universally necessary aspect of sexual citizenship. As we shall see in chapter 7, for example, being out is simply not an option for some groups of sexual citizens, such as immigrants.

One aspect of Butler's note of caution that we would like to signal here, then, is the *global* unevenness in available and affordable options for sexual citizens. Given the growing importance of transnational capital, it is perhaps inevitable that the arguments around gay consumption have looked at the impact of globalization on the pink economy. In some of this work, there is an unfortunate tendency to construct gay consumer culture as globally homogeneous. For instance, David Evans equates gay consumption with a particular form of global culture, citing consumption practices such as international gay tourism as proof of a homogeneous capital culture:

> In this sense there clearly *is* specifically homosexual consumption in a global gay market and it is largely in this sense that the 'international gay community' with common norms and values exists. One doesn't know of course just how part-time the gay tourists' participation in solely gay territories is, but there is no doubt that the material discourses on homosexuality have, with modest provisos over local constraints on the expression of these subcultural values, effectively reduced the world to the dimensions of Earls Court or Christopher Street, which is no mean feat.   (1993, p. 113)

As we shall see in chapter 7, the globalizing of gay identity and politics is itself a matter for considerable unease, especially when globalization is seen as a mode of western economic and cultural (as well as sexual) imperialism. What this means is that the ever-shifting 'finanscapes' of the global economy (Appadurai, 1996) will continue to have (often unpredictable) impacts on the experiences and political struggles that make up sexual citizenship.

Nothing to offer?

This chapter has examined the discourses surrounding the pink economy in the light of the growing marketization and commodification of citizenship. We noted that some writers condemn lesbian and gay consumption practices in a highly moralistic manner, while other commentators have argued that lesbian and gay rights can be conceived as a commodity to be bought and sold on the open market; thus capitalism can actually secure lesbian and gay liberation. Both arguments are equally problematic. The latter echoes Harper's (1997) critique of Andrew Sullivan's *Virtually Normal* – that the assimilationist wing of lesbian and gay politics will secure freedom for some, but not for all: the shopping list of rights carries a price tag that exceeds some sexual citizens' financial means, as Barbara Smith highlights. Those arguments that reject the market as a political space, however, seem to demand the jettisoning of any possibility of using the strategies of consumer citizenship, devaluing the growing centrality of consumption to the articulation of identity and politics.

What we need is a more nuanced discussion of consumption practices, such as that provided by Peter Cohen (1997) in his essay on AIDS, class and consumption among middle-class gay men involved in ACT UP. Cohen's carefully positioned paper points a way for a critically informed perspective on the economics of sexual citizenship – one that avoids simplistic narratives of consumption as liberation, or victimization, or pathology. He notes that for middle-class white gay men, the AIDS crisis has been experienced as a 'class dislocation'; AIDS not only restricted the capacity of certain (closeted) gay men to pass as straight, but moreover it has displaced them from their position within the dominant classes by stigmatizing them. His story neatly highlights the complex and shifting interrelationships between class and sexuality, reminding us that our discussions should themselves reflect that complexity and uncertainty.

Moreover, we need a less phobic and less naive discussion of the distinctive relationships between sexuality and consumption. While some commentators champion the growth of the gay market, many gay consumers remain unmoved and rather bemused by all the targeting and niche-marketing. In addition, the growth of new venues (taken as a barometer of gay economic power – and of its exploitation) is not welcomed with open arms by all. The homogeneity, attitude and high prices of some venues is surely nothing new to anyone on the gay scene. People are not duped by the hype surrounding new venues, but instead have a love/hate relationship towards them. Consumers know they are being targeted and exploited, but knowing that the rules of the game are rigged does not stop them using the scene. Users of gay venues are like the audience in professional wrestling, so lovingly discussed by Roland Barthes (1973) in *Mythologies*; we know the game is fixed but we attend for the spectacle: 'The public is completely uninterested in knowing whether the contest is rigged or not, and rightly so; it abandons itself to the primary virtue of the spectacle, which is to abolish all motives and all consequences: what matters is not what it thinks but what it sees' (p. 15).

Debates over the role of gay villages in promoting economic visibility need to be located in this kind of context: they simultaneously prove that economic muscle (or at least perceived economic muscle) may bring about real material change, but at the same time remind us that such change is neither available to nor welcomed by everyone in the 'target market'. It's not as simple as saying that gay bars necessarily combat homophobia, or as arguing that participating in the pink economy is always an unprincipled sell-out. Gay villages are the consumer-citizen's version of the earlier political strategy founded on gay neighbourhoods as voting blocs. As a spatial concentration of sexual dissidents, they make visible particular forms of power (whether economic or electoral) that can effect change at the level of policy – for example, when cities use gay space as part of a marketing strategy based on selling diversity. Patterns of exclusion inevitably mark such a strategy, however: not everyone can afford the high prices in trendy new gay bars, just as not everyone can afford to live in gentrified gay neighbourhoods. While 'trickle-down' arguments might suggest that in the end such strategies will benefit everyone, regardless of whether or not they directly participate, we have to be mindful of the fickle nature of the market, and of the limits of what such a marketized politics can and cannot achieve.

Crucially, in thinking about consumer citizenship in relation to sexuality, we need to move beyond simplistic discussions of why gay men (and lesbians) shop, and part of this corrective must be to trace the evolution of lesbian and gay consumption practices in relation to the familial orientation of the welfare state. The major reason that the market has provided the stage for the realization of lesbian and gay identities has been the heterosexualization of the welfare state. In addition, we have to recognize the heterosexual-ization of aspects of consumption, especially those that now stand in for the welfare state. As Russell Child argues, the family unit has been the assumed basis for such aspects of consumption:

> Even if some white gay men are indeed relatively wealthy, this does not necessarily mean that they are economically better off than their heterosexual counterparts, because some types of consumption are more expensive for consumers who are not part of a traditional heterosexual family unit. This is for example the case in sections of the housing market, and also in the market for pensions and other personal insurance cover, where most products are tailored towards the interests of traditional family units. It should be noted that the same higher prices also apply for lesbians, for lesbian and gay adolescents, for black lesbians and gay men, and for people who for example have had their careers blocked after being open about their homosexuality.   (1993, pp. 172–3)

Until very recently, the welfare state sought to reproduce only heterosexuality and to penalize sexual diversity. A more thorough examination of the heteronormativity of the welfare state is long overdue, therefore, and must serve as a counter to the rather misleading media and academic commentary on the state of the pink economy. An awareness of the economic basis of sexual citizenship is thus essential to the discussions throughout *The Sexual Citizen*. We have already argued that the city is the primary locale for the struggles over sexual citizenship, and debates over the location of lesbian and gay businesses inevitably have an urban focus (just as the urban geography of sex zones is overwritten by economics). Likewise, the economic bases of love and the romantic tradition must be acknowledged – something that the arguments over lesbian and gay marriage must attend to. Even debates such as that on gays in the military have an economic aspect, as we have already seen, given the fact that joining the armed forces might be one of the only available ways for working-class queers to escape an isolated and oppressive home life (Lee Badget, 1997b). In short, our suggestion is that the economics of sexual citizenship are far more complex and multifaceted than the kinds of analysis provided thus far have accounted for.

7

Transnational Sexual Citizenship

Turning the love that dared not speak its name into 'families we choose' or 'alternative families', 'love we frame' or 'alternative love' or even that most fraught move the 'love that knows no borders', cannot extricate us from the tendency of love to return us to Nation, to a nation that would rather maintain itself as the central love object than give all its people the tools they need to survive an epidemic.

Cindy Patton, ' "On me, not in me": locating affect in nationalism after AIDS'

The literature on formations of citizenship frequently stresses the centrality of the nation as the citizenship-space that citizens primarily belong to. We need, therefore, to be mindful that, despite the universalizing rhetoric of citizenship (at least in the context of late-modern liberal democracies), there are clear *national differences* in the ways that citizenship works. Moreover, we must consider the extent to which political strategies around citizenship are inevitably shaped by the national contexts in which they arise: can modes of activism embodied, for example, in queer politics be mobilized successfully outside of the USA? In this context, Carl Stychin (1998, p. 21) notes that 'the construction of rights in the United States represents a particular balance of interests, one that is not necessarily replicated in other rights cultures'. The enshrining of rights discourse in the US Constitution, and its materialization in law and politics, means for Stychin that identity politics is effectively 'legalized' in the USA, in the sense that law is seen as the principal political site for rights struggles. The US model of rights-based 'legalized' politics cannot work in nation-states where the foundations of citizenship are differently constructed – in the UK, for example, the rights claims of sexual citizens are inseparable from the new right's colonization of the discourse of citizenship in the Citizen's Charter (Evans, 1993). In contrasting British formations of sexual citizenship with those of the United States, we are equally aware that Britishness is a concept that has never been more contested – national identities are not themselves static, but get recast in line with changes both within the nation-state and in its relation to the wider world. These transatlantic differences in political structures and formations of citizenship are mirrored in the different ways that academics have approached the study of sexual citizenship, as well as in the strategies that activists mobilize. In this chapter we bring these tensions into focus by examining the changing place of the nation in formations of sexual citizenship.

As Yasemin Soysal notes, the symbolic articulation of 'nation' remains a powerful motif in claims for rights and recognition:

> The idea of the nation becomes a trope of convenience for claims to collective rights and identity. Even groups that may not fit the classic definitions of a nation refer to themselves as such: gays and lesbians claim a 'Queer Nation'...In this universalizing flux, the ways of 'doing identity'...become standardized exercises, with common themes and modes of presentation.   (1994, p. 161)

As Carl Stychin (1998) shows, the nation continues to be the most legible frame for rights claims to be articulated within. However, in the light of the transformative processes of globalization, we must also be aware of the limitations of nation-based formulations of citizenship. We have to consider challenges to established theories of nation-centred citizenship from writers who discuss a global or cosmopolitan mode of citizenship, or who articulate a postnational model of citizenship. In doing so, we must state at the outset that we do not accept that the nation-state has become redundant as the primary basis of sexual citizenship. Indeed the comparative work of Jan Willem Duyvendak (1996) on gay rights movements and political structures in France and the Netherlands points towards a more nuanced consideration of national differences both in the regulation of sexualities and in sexual cultures themselves, rather than vague statements about globalization. While there have been arguments that read globalization as homogenizing gay culture, identity and politics, work on national identity and sexuality continues to remind us of the importance of the nation in the context of sexual citizenship. Movement across national borders brings us into contact with these national contexts, reminding us that borders serve many purposes in defining citizenship – a central issue we shall return to later in this chapter.

In other contexts, the transnationalization process has brought sexual citizenship into new domains. As Stychin notes, the 'globalization of law' – for example, through the discourse of universal human rights – shifts the terrain of conflict for rights struggles away from an exclusive focus on the nation-state, although the relationship between national and transnational forces is a complex and uneven one, with appeals to 'global' rights working better in some countries than in others, where extra-national intervention provokes nationalist counterdiscourses (think of the UK's relationship to the European Union). In an attempt to think through the role of the national and the transnational in sexual citizenship, we want to focus first on the nation-state, and on 'New Britain' – the articulation of national identity and culture spearheaded by Tony Blair's Labour administration. To do this we will focus first on the place of the welfare state in notions of Britishness; as we noted in chapter 4, social citizenship is predicated on access to welfare, and the creation of the British welfare state enshrines this dimension of social inclusion/exclusion. The 'full' British citizen is guaranteed welfare rights; as Diane Richardson (1998) points out, lesbians' and gay men's limited access to welfare thus marks them as only 'partial' citizens.

New Britain?

As we have noted already, the British welfare state was produced and is sustained by heterosexualized discourses around the fixed boundaries of both the family and the nation-state. Writers such as Fiona Williams (1992) have suggested that the postwar British welfare state was established on the basis of the promotion of the family unit and the defence and protection of white Britishness, and that the discourses around the current crises in the restructuring of the welfare state are similarly sexualized (and racialized). The Blair government's policies on welfare and citizenship still carry strong moral overtones. While Tony Blair has carefully sought to distance himself from homophobia in his pro-family agenda, the strong central New Labour message – about the need to promote family and community as the basis of a revived British nationalism – is bound to cause alarm to sexual dissidents (among others).

Anna Marie Smith (1994) has shown that, in the 1980s, the pro-family values agenda of the British new right mobilized an explicit, forcefully promoted homophobia, especially through Section 28 of the Local Government Act, which prohibited the promotion of homosexuality as a 'pretended family relationship'. New Labour ostensibly recognizes the value of lesbian and gay relationships; nevertheless, the family remains the centrepiece in social policy and welfare discussions under Blair, with the ideology of the family working metonymically for the nation:

> It is in the family that we first learn to negotiate the boundaries of acceptable conduct and to recognise that we owe responsibilities to others as well as to ourselves. We then build out from that family base to the community, and beyond it to society as a whole. The values of a decent society are in many ways the values of the family unit, which is why helping to re-establish good family and community life should be a central objective of government policy. And that cannot be achieved without policies – especially in respect of employment and education – that improve society as a whole. (Blair, 1996, p. 247)

It is therefore necessary to link changes in the definition and politics of the family to changes in nationalism, especially in this case British nationalism. Something is happening to British nationalism under Blair: the new moral order of New Labour is intimately linked to the changing position of the UK within the global economy, and specifically to anxieties linked to Europeanization and globalization. Blair has repeatedly stressed family and community as necessary protection from the individualizing self-interest of the marketplace. Moreover, New Labour's view of a strong community as the bulwark against social disintegration champions the nation, for the nation is the strong community envisaged by Blair. Spatial scales are significant here, because Blair is often vague on what he means by community: community is used sometimes to denote localities, at other times to denote the nation – New Britain. Some commentators argue that New Labour has meant a radical 're-vision' of British nationalism, that New Labour has expounded a New Britain founded on a new national self-confidence, embodied in terms like 'Cool Britannia', which stands in part for a new 'progressive' British nationalism that embraces cultural diversity and pluralism. However, as Beth Edginton (1998) argues in an essay on the death of Princess Diana, the government's response to that 'national crisis' served to highlight the fragility of this new vision of the UK. Meanwhile, in their searching analysis of New Labour, Driver and Martell note how community, nation and state have become blurred in Blair's thinking about the rights and responsibilities of the citizen:

> Labour modernizers like to talk up *community responsibilities* and the *power of the community*, but often fall short of identifying exactly what agency is to carry those responsibilities or exercise that power. In the absence of detailed policy proposals, there remains a nagging doubt that *community* may just be a synonym for the *state*. (1997, p. 36, emphasis in original)

Moreover, they detect a strong undertone of nationalism – based on common values and sameness rather than difference – in Blair's vision, and a redrafting of the 'local' focus of communitarianism that restates the national as the local in what they call Blair's 'One-Nation discourse' and new social morality; both are powerful articulations of citizenship in New Britain.

So, according to Driver and Martell, the reality of Blair's 'One-Nation' vision is bound up with a set of proscriptions about what is acceptable behaviour – a moral conformity. The rationale for this moral conformity, according to Blair, is the need for the UK to prosper in what he terms the 'new global economy'. Blair makes explicit the link between his championing of a new morality for the UK and the country's success in the global economy when he states that 'I believe in what I call one-nation politics: that social cohesion and fairness to all are essential conditions of both a decent and an efficient country. Only in this way can we persuade our people to live and thrive in the new global economy' (Blair, 1996, p. 128). It is important, therefore, to consider the ways in which New Britain is located within the contexts of both the global economy and Europe, since a reorienting of the nation towards the wider world has been a central aim of New Labour – and one that has crucial impacts for sexual citizenship, both positively and negatively.

Britain, Europe and the World

Globalization is perhaps one of the most significant contexts and discourses in framing the discussion of welfare reform and social policy in general. Tony Blair's project of building New Britain seeks to address the problem of an underachieving workforce and the UK's failing competitiveness in the global economy. The education of the workforce is essential for New Britain – but in order to bring this about, the country needs to become more efficient. Thus Clarke and Newman (1997, p. 46) make clear the link between globalization discourse and the growth of the managerialist state, writing that '[t]he development of a global economy has formed one of the meta-narratives which has legitimized change, at the level of the state itself and in terms of the management of organizations'. However, they recognize that there is politics of spatial scale at work here, and that certain scales privilege certain questions and issues. Choosing to focus on one scale for framing any discussion of a problem or issue inevitably means that other perspectives on a situation are excluded or silenced. They note, for example, that local agency tends to disappear when issues are framed at the global scale. For Clarke and Newman, the local is the point at which power is acutely felt, and they argue that globalization is used ideologically to reinforce structural and organizational changes at the local scale. Moreover, the discourse of globalization promotes a profound sense of economic insecurity that purportedly undermines our sense of self-identity. In this sense the promotion of the communitarian ethic in New Labour points in fact towards a new conservatism – the search for an impossible stability in an unstable world.

Paisley Currah (1995) argues that lesbians' and gay men's desire for immutability, for certainty – in the appeal to essentialist notions of identity, for example – must be seen as unsurprising given the uncertainties that confront everyday life for lesbians and gay men. Thus the hard choices we are faced with are made fuzzy by the ethic of managerialism that arises out of the nation-state's attempt to provide an anchor in the face of globalization. As sexual citizens we are all encouraged to manage ourselves, manage our consumerism, manage our bodies. The only control and security we have is mediated via the market, yet this is also profoundly unstable and a source of tremendous anxiety. While globalization is not to blame *per se* for our current state of insecurity, Burkitt and Ashton (1996) argue that it can work against the very social cohesion Blair is attempting to foster. Against this backdrop, communitarianism and other ideologies that promise security and stability obviously seem appealing. Even Tony Blair mentions (albeit in passing) the costs of globalization – and notes that social and moral uncertainties are related to processes of globalization:

> The mirror image of the economic insecurity is a profound sense of social, even moral, insecurity. This is not the place to explore this issue, but I do believe that this too is linked to globalisation. Work patterns have changed; expectations have radically altered; the old cultural, social and family ties have loosened. Communities which previously changed little from one generation to the next have collapsed. Belief in religion has diminished. Crime, antisocial behaviour, irresponsibility have all increased. There is no point in taking refuge in nostalgia, but we have not yet learned how to handle and make sense of these changes.   (Blair, 1996, p. 121)

As a commentary on detraditionalization, Blair's expression of anxiety again legitimates the role of the nation-state as a site of security – but this comes at a price, in terms of establishing a modality of national belonging and consensus that cannot accommodate difference, as long as difference bears the mark of uncertainty and insecurity. Globalization can, then, provoke the articulation of a defensive nationalism, mobilizing divisive forms of social exclusion.

Linked to globalization in the UK context, as we have already mentioned, is the Europeanization of issues of equality and citizenship. A number of writers point towards this process as an uneven one, speculating about the form and direction that the future Europeanization of sexual justice may take (Tatchell, 1992; Duy-vendak, 1994, 1995, 1996; Waaldijk and Chapman, 1993). What this uneven and tentative process towards the formation of a European sexual citizenship demonstrates is the limits of thinking about sexual citizenship in terms of the nation-state (Binnie, 1997). In particular, the Labour government's free vote on the reduction of the age of consent for gay men to sixteen, in June 1998, was to some extent motivated by the prospect of likely defeat in the European courts if the UK Parliament voted against reform. Interestingly, Clarke and Newman (1997) point towards Europeanization in decision-making around questions of equality and fairness as reflective of a crisis in trust in British political institutions, and the failure of the managerialist approach to manage competing claims on the welfare state. Of course, as the cases of Lisa Grant and the Operation Spanner men so vividly illustrate, turning to Europe for justice offers absolutely no guarantees.[1] Moreover, it is imperative that we recognize that claims for sexual citizenship are predicated on the exclusion of others. For instance, European sexual citizenship may provide a greater array of rights (and obligations) for European lesbians and gay men, but excluded from this evolving status are those sexual non-citizens who do not conform to western sexual categories, and who are barred from entry to the European Union.

Thus far in this chapter we have traced New Labour's project of a New Britain, and the ways in which Europeanization and globalization have reshaped British national identity. We have argued that Blair has mobilized discourses of globalization to legitimate welfare reform and the vigorous promotion of the family – projects that profoundly impact on the sexual citizen. However, globalization is working in other ways in relation to sexual citizenship, most notably in the evolution of a transnational sexual politics. As Isin and Wood (1999, p. 156) put it, 'globalization cuts both ways. While it may be weakening the nation-state, it is also opening up new spaces for groups to enact new types of politics.' In the light of this, Yasemin Soysal (1994) has argued for a *postnational* model for citizenship, noting that the globalization of a universal human rights discourse which privileges the individual makes the nation-state less relevant as an actor in determining the rights and obligations of citizenship (see also Cohen, 1999). Is the nation-state therefore becoming less significant as an era of globalized citizenship?

Towards a globalized sexual citizenship?

Some critics argue that globalization has led to the export of western definitions of sexual practices, identities and cultures around the world. In some circles there is the highly problematic notion of the 'global gay identity', which Dennis Altman (1996, p. 77) defines as 'the apparent internationalization of a certain form of social and cultural identity based upon homosexuality'. This global gay identity presupposes a common unifying experience of homophobia – in the same way that the women's movement mobilized a notion of shared oppression in the catch-phrase 'Sisterhood is global' (a slogan later critiqued for totalizing 'woman' and thereby neglecting the local dimension of women's oppression and feminist struggle). As we discussed earlier gay identity is being increasingly forged through consumption practices, and this is particularly the case in international tourism and the development of global gay tourist destinations such as San Francisco, Sydney, New York, Amsterdam, London and Paris. Bob Cant fears that the emergence of a global pink economy is based upon uniformity and conformity:

> The spread of McDonald's has been noted as one of the main results of the globalization of the economy. What could emerge for the lesbian and gay communities is the spread of McPink – a global pink economy which promotes a series of ever-changing lifestyle options. The pink economy could be the unaccountable motor of a new conformity that packages the desirable and rejects those who do not fit in as vigorously as did any traditional community. (1997, p. 11)

In this vision of a globalized McPink economy, sameness is asserted over difference between and among lesbians and gay men. Marginalized from this globalized McPink economy are those who are trapped in poverty, unable to buy into the 'global gay lifestyle'. While this argument unproblematically assumes that globalization always produces sameness, denying local recontextualizations that to some extent 'indigenize' and rework homogeneous global forms as well as overlooking the diversity of local frames of meaning across transnational space (see Jackson, 1999), there are serious implications for sexual citizenship that must be recognized here, if there is a danger in exporting a mode of 'being gay' from late-modern westernized liberal democracies that does in fact 'McDonaldize' sexual minorities.

Arjun Appadurai's (1996) famous formulation of globalization as a network of 'disjunctive flows' is useful for thinking about global sexual citizenship. For Appadurai, globalization is a complex, almost chaotic process, with movements of people, images, technologies, money and ideologies criss-crossing the world, sometimes in unison and sometimes in contradiction. We can use this model to think about Cant's McDonaldization argument, for instance, by considering 'mediascapes' (dominant representations of homosexuality) and 'ideoscapes' (such as post-Stonewall lesbian and gay rights) and their reception in particular contexts. For example, in his landmark essay 'In the shadows of Stonewall' (1995), Martin Manalansan IV argues that the 'Stonewall myth' of the emergence of 'modern' gay identity and gay liberation has come to represent a global gay identity that inevitably masks difference. He stresses that the voices of the Filipino men in his research are marginalized by the myth of post-Stonewall global gay identity, a myth that has also been taken to task by Dennis Altman:

> The romantic myth of homosexual identity cutting across class, race, and so on doesn't work in practice any more than it does in the West. The experience of sexuality in everyday life is shaped by such variables as the gap between city and country; ethnic and religious differences; and hierarchies of wealth, education, and age. The idea of a gay or lesbian/gay community assumed that such differences can be subordinated to an overarching sense of sexual identity, a myth that is barely sustainable in comparatively rich and affluent societies. (1996, p. 89)

It is this notion of a universal gay identity based on a common experience of homophobia that gives credibility and legitimacy to western academics' research on non-western sexual cultures. As Stychin (1998, p. 196) remarks, there is 'a danger of colonization

by an Anglo-American model of [sexual] identity' in formulations
that universalize issues of sexual citizenship. A number of leading
lights in lesbian and gay studies have attempted to articulate how
sexual cultures are being transformed by globalizing processes. For
instance, consider Gilbert Herdt's *Same Sex: Different Cultures*
(1997) and Alan Sinfield's essay on the queer diaspora (Sinfield,
1996).

Herdt constructs himself as the all-knowing cosmopolitan gay
intellectual – an anthropological expert and authority on non-
western sexual cultures. The blurb for his book *Same Sex, Different
Cultures* states that he lives in Chicago and Amsterdam, as if to add
to his position as a commentator on global gay culture. He uses
terms such as 'unsophisticated' to describe non-metropolitan North
America, and continually attempts to shoe-horn his anthropological observations of same-sex practices into a model of 'gay behaviour' legibile only in the modern West, assuming that sexual
cultures based on a western model will develop as the places he
visits mature or modernize – that is, when they become sophistic-
ated. Alan Sinfield, meanwhile, attempts to map queer subjectivities
on to postcolonial theories of hybridity and diaspora; however, like
Herdt his analysis proceeds problematically. In Sinfield's essay the
'gay subject' is assumed to be 'white'; moreover, he contrasts
the gay diaspora with the African diaspora in a way that renders
black queers invisible:

> for lesbians and gay men the diasporic sense of separation and loss,
> so far from affording a principle of coherence for our subcultures,
> may actually attach to aspects of the (heterosexual) culture of our
> childhood, where we are no longer 'at home'. Instead of dispersing,
> we assemble. The hybridity of our subcultures derives not from the
> loss of even a mythical unity, but from the difficulty we experience in
> envisioning ourselves beyond the framework of normative hetero-
> sexism. . . . If diasporic Africans are poised between alternative home-
> lands – in mid-Atlantic, Gilroy suggests – then lesbians and gay men
> are stuck at the moment of emergence. For coming out is not once-
> and-for-all; like the Africans, we never quite arrive.   (1996, p. 282)

As part of his search for the queer diaspora, Sinfield looks to
Simon Watney's essay on the same subject, which states that the
nearest equivalent to a queer diasporic experience 'is the sense of

relief and safety which a gay man or lesbian finds in a gay bar or a dyke bar in a strange city in a foreign country. Even if one cannot speak the local language, we feel a sense of identification' (Watney, 1995, p. 61). In this brief aside, Watney problematically presupposes the western gay male subject as mobile and affluent and western – the western tourist looking for comfort in a 'strange city in a foreign country' – whereas other sexual dissidents who are located differently within what Doreen Massey (1995) terms the 'power-space geometry' of time-space compression, are trapped in space, lacking the mobility to participate in international tourism. The comforting sameness of gay bar life that Watney celebrates is a prominent manifestation of 'global gay identity', offering a home away from home for the tourist. However, we should also be mindful of Jackson's (1999) observation that this assumed homogeneity masks a multitude of local differences. And, returning to Appadurai's global flows, we should remember that his 'ethnoscapes' (movements of people) contain not just tourists – who, it must be said, articulate a very particular relationship to globalization – but also migrants, refugees and exiles: groups who move because they have to. The flows of these groups follow a very different trajectory from that mapped by the global gay jet-set; a trajectory steered by policies on migration and settlement originating at the scale of the nation-state.

Migration and sexual citizenship

Nothing throws the question of the different ways in which formations of sexual citizenship are constructed by nation-states into greater relief than migration policies. Migration brings into focus the degree to which the boundaries of the nation are open or closed to sexualized others. For instance, Carl Stychin (1998, p. 162) notes the importance of law reform in the area of immigration policy in Australia, arguing that 'it is significant that a national culture so centrally informed by migration, journeys, and (increasingly) multiculturalism created a space for successful activist struggles around gay and lesbian immigration'. By contrast, Eithne Luibheid (1998, p. 504), writing on the current status of lesbians and gay men in US immigration policy, paints a very different picture there, suggesting that lesbians and gay men are still routinely excluded on the grounds that they lack good moral character. In addition, they cannot use long-term relationships with US citizens or residents as a basis for claiming their own US residency (a right that is available to opposite-sex couples). And, of course, once within the USA, lesbians and gay men are faced with endemic homophobia. Further, in her essay on the sexualization of the border between the USA and Mexico, Jessica Chapin notes that anti-immigration discourses mobilize homophobic imagery in a way that makes dissident sexualities represent a threat to the US nationhood:

> Anxieties about undocumented immigrants are often expressed in terms that suggest a homosexualization of US-Mexico relations, an inversion of hierarchies. The threat of anal penetration, a loosening of the sphincter in order to let something in instead of to push something out, is homophobically cast as a perversion of the 'natural' order and a threat to the social order. (1998, p. 413)

In this sense all immigrants to the USA, not just lesbians and gay men, are sexualized, since the national body itself takes on a (hetero)sexualized form (Patton, 1999).

The increasing recognition of same-sex relationships for the purpose of immigration, residency and citizenship in some national contexts is significant and put into context by Yasemin Soysal (1994), who argues that while western nation-states have increasingly sought to restrict immigration, the expansion and adoption of universal rights means that asylum has become a possibility for more and more groups – at least in theory. One strand of this argument in the context of sexual citizenship would be that, since citizenship is being increasingly expressed through the logic of the market (including the labour market), affluent professional lesbians and gay men with marketable skills stand a much greater chance of realizing transnational citizenship than others. However, this argument not only reinforces the stereotyping of lesbians and gay men as 'footloose' and affluent, it also hides the dominant way in which immigration as a 'right' depends on specific 'responsibilities'. One constant in migration policy for sexual citizens is an emphasis on long-term monogamous relationships: same-sex couples must prove that their relationships are stable. Moreover, the law recognizes only a very small fraction of the diversity of sexual relationships and erotic possibilities by drawing up categories for inclusion and exclusion: 'The incorporation of sexual categorizations into exclusion laws, as well as the development of procedures to detect and deter entry by those who fit the categorizations, is a key piece of how the immigration system came to exclude individuals on the basis of sexuality' (Luibheid, 1998, pp. 479–80).

While gay men may be excluded on the basis of their sexuality, gender differences are also significant, making gay men more mobile than lesbians in the first place – though both face multiple possibilities for exclusion. In the homophobic constructions of nationhood, lesbians remain invisible, even though Luibheid reminds us that 'it is important to emphasize that lesbians do cross borders' (p. 501). This invisibilizing works in many ways. Given the restrictions placed on prospective immigrants, *passing* becomes a necessary strategy for gaining and sustaining inclusion. Chapin (1998) uses Judith Butler's notion of performativity to examine the ways in which inclusion and exclusion work out in terms of passing. She notes the ways in which Mexican immigrants to the USA dress to pass: 'Like the homosexual, the undocumented immigrant opens an epistemological gap by exercising the power to dissemble, to pass. The possibility that aliens might pass successfully as Americans signals the presence of an indistinguishable difference within the United States and recasts the national self, rather than the Mexican other, as a problem of knowledge' (p. 414).

This is significant for, as Cindy Patton has argued, we embody our nation when we travel across national borders. Our citizenship is marked on our bodies – hence the immigrant's need to pass, to remain undetected. However, the possibility of movement across national borders is not open to all sexual dissidents equally, as we have already noted. Thus we need to make visible the role played by borders in excluding queers who cannot pass. Gayatri Gopinath argues that for South Asians the question of full citizenship rights is complicated by belonging in multiple national spaces:

> As queer South Asians in the diaspora, 'citizenship,' queer or otherwise, is not something that we can ever take for granted. Rather, we enact a much more complicated navigation of state regulatory

> practices and *multiple* national spaces – one that is often profoundly
> mobile, contingent, and evasive, and that demands a more nuanced
> theorization of the interplay of state and nation.   (1996, pp. 120–1)

Gopinath also takes to task theorists of sexual citizenship such as
Berlant and Freedman (1993), who state that disidentification with
US nationality is not an option for queer citizens. Gopinath argues
that this overlooks the fact that *identification* with either nationality
or citizenship is not an option for many queers (particularly queers
of colour) in the USA. Gopinath's critique of the ethnocentricity of
discussions of sexual citizenship is especially significant here, given
the increased interest in theorizing sexualities at the global or
transnational level. What this points to is the need to be wary of
importing a westernized reading of globalization in relation to sexual citizenship. The complexities of national, transnational and
global identifications and disidentifications thus produce their own
disjunctive flows around the world, mapping out the complex
implications that globalization has upon sexual citizenship.

8

Turn it into Love

The possibility of intimacy means the promise of democracy.
Anthony Giddens, *The Transformation of Intimacy*

We have to understand that with our desires, through our desires, go new forms of relationships, new forms of love, new forms of creation.
Michel Foucault, 'Sex, power, and the politics of identity'

There has been a noticeable turn towards love in recent writings on sexual politics, and it seems appropriate here to think through calls, such as Giddens', to work through the politics of intimacy and link that to democracy (and to citizenship). Remember that the end-point of Ken Plummer's (1995) sexual storytelling is the creation of a zone of 'intimate citizenship', which includes new forms of relationship; similarly, one of the central preconditions that gives rise to the possiblity of the sexual citizen for Jeffrey Weeks (1999) is what he calls the 'democratization' of love. In Lauren Berlant's short essay, introducing a special issue of *Critical Inquiry* on the theme of intimacy, a similar motif appears: 'stories of the intimate have become inseparable from ... stories about citizenship' (1998, p. 288). For Giddens (1992, p. 190), the place to begin recasting democracy is not in the public sphere, but in the sphere of the intimate; note that he uses the vocabulary of citizenship to talk about intimacy: 'Rights and obligations: as I have tried to make clear, in some part these define what intimacy actually is. Intimacy should not be understood as an interactional description, but as a cluster of prerogatives and responsibilities that define agendas of practical activity'.

In his tracing of love relations in 'modern' societies, Giddens arrives at the conclusion that the growing self-autonomy in relationships inevitably has implications for democratizing relations outside the couple: learning to love means learning to be a democratic citizen (for a critical reading of Giddens on love, see Jamieson (1999)). It is here that some of the principal tensions explored in this chapter (and elsewhere) begin to complicate these rallying cries for intimate citizenship: How can we think about intimacy without reinstating the public/private divide; without keeping intimacy's link to privacy intact? How do we think love in ways other than those hegemonically scripted by mainstream culture? What is it that we talk about when we talk about love?

It is clear from a glance across the critical literature on intimacy that there are countless ways to think and talk about love. Its relation to sex, its relation to romance, its relation to friendship – let alone its relation to democracy or citizenship – get worked over in many radically different ways. We want to begin, then, by commenting on some of this academic writing on intimacy, before moving on to think through in more detail the links between love (in its many forms – romance, friendship, family) and sexual citizenship; to sketch, then, some of what Susan Bickford (1997, p. 125) calls 'the passions of citizenship'.

Love in the academy

It is not our purpose here to provide an exhaustive survey of critical and theoretical approaches to intimacy. Instead, we offer a mere dalliance with some recent writings on love, chiefly as a way of foregrounding our own attempts to think about 'intimate citizenship', to assess the use value of such a notion. And perhaps the first striking thing to notice about love in the academy is the kinds of stylistic flourish it brings from the hands (and hearts) of scholars – despite (or perhaps because of) Sally Munt's (1998, p. 18) assertion that love is 'a contentious term to evoke, a discomforting concept within an academic work'. We are struck by the kinds of approach to love that we find in texts exploring its myths and meanings: from

the aphoristic (Barthes, 1977/1990; Phillips, 1996) to the therapeutic (Giddens, 1992); from the intertextual (Barsky, 1994) to the
confessional (Kipnis, 1998; Sedgwick, 1998). Of course, we also
find more sober scholarship, such as Steven Seidman's tracing of
love's American history in *Romantic Longings* (1991), or critical
work exposing love's contradictions and complicities (as in some
essays in the collection *Romance Revisited*, edited by Lynne Pearce
and Jackie Stacey (1995); or the more strident attack on love's
oppressions to be found in Nicola Field's *Over the Rainbow*
(1995)). Most notably, in these texts and in others, such as Ulrich
Beck and Elisabeth Beck-Gernsheim's *The Normal Chaos of Love*
(1995) or Eva Illouz's *Consuming the Romantic Utopia* (1997), we
find love intertwined with capitalism – marketized, commodified,
bought and sold. What are we to make of all this? How can we find
a way through all this love talk, and what can we take from it to
begin the task of thinking intimacy as democracy? What do we
mean – to borrow a phrase from David Oswell (1998) – by 'true
love in queer times'?

In particular, we need to attend to the dominant scripting of love
in terms of long-term monogamous heterosexual pairing –
inscribed and legitimated in the institution of marriage (see also
chapter 3). There is plenty of work, most notably by feminist
scholars, which seeks to critique marriage as the bedrock of patriarchal domination (e.g. O'Donovan, 1993); nevertheless, as we
have already seen, marriage remains the centrepiece for models of
romantic attachment, and the task of thinking love otherwise can
be a tricky one. Finding a way to recast love outside of the couple-
form requires some creative accounting, some leaps of imagination.
As Lauren Berlant writes:

> desires for intimacy that bypass the couple or the life narratives it
> generates have no alternative plots, let alone few laws and stable
> spaces of culture in which to clarify and cultivate them . . . To rethink
> intimacy is to appraise how we have been and how we live and how
> we might imagine lives that make more sense than the ones so many
> are living. (1998, pp. 285–6)

Now, this does not mean that we have to jettison notions of love
totally; as Stevi Jackson (1995, p. 50) says, '[i]t is not necessary to

deny the pleasures of romance or the euphoria of falling in love in order to be sceptical about romantic ideals and wary of their consequences'. Charting the social construction of love – and its codification in discourses of 'romance' – is an essential step towards giving substance to that scepticism and wariness, and from there to imagine love outside of those limited and limiting discourses. And we find ourselves in a contradictory time in this respect: at once those discourses are being shored up by forms of social remoralization, but they are also being undermined as their ideological undergirdings become more transparent. As both *The Transformation of Intimacy* and *The Normal Chaos of Love* make clear (albeit in rather different ways and with rather different agendas), there have been fundamental changes in modes of love and loving in late-modern, detraditionalized societies; 'the contradictions of romantic love', Jackson (1995, p. 59) writes, 'are becoming more apparent with the partial erosion of its institutional supports'.

Let's stay with Giddens and Beck and Beck-Gernsheim a little longer, for here we have two important texts reflecting on love under the contradictory conditions sketched above – two texts that seek to rework love in the face of new uncertainties. Both attest to the continued desire for love – indeed, both find this desire heightened in the wake of the social transformations of our age. Both acknowledge that, to a lesser or greater extent, the familiar scripts of love are becoming outmoded, and that new times call for new romance: 'Love is becoming a blank that the lovers must fill in themselves, across the widening trenches of biography, even if they are directed by the lyrics of pop songs, advertisements, pornographic scripts, light fiction or psychoanalysis' (Beck and Beck-Gernsheim, 1995, p. 5).

Despite their similar starting-points, however, the two texts veer off from one another dramatically thenceforth. Drawing on therapeutic love-work, Giddens formulates his modern romance around notions such as 'confluent love' – love that resists the foreverness of marriage, that is consensually contracted, and that need not be combined with sexual fidelity, the exclusive couple-form, or modelled on the heterosexual family. Giddens' openness to considering homosexual relationships as offering lessons in love that heterosexuals might wish to follow is welcome and problematic simultaneously: for while it attests to his desire to see beyond the heterosexual couple, it leads him into romanticizing queers as pioneers of 'pure' relationships, without problematizing same-sex intimacy by considering issues of power, violence and exploitation that can reside there as much as in hetero-intimacy. However, while his accounts of lesbian and gay male relationships are held at a distance, he is nonetheless able and willing to draw very positive conclusions from the diversity of intimate arrangements sketched out, at least in the sense that they expand the possible scripts of intimacy. In considering 'episodic sexuality' (so-called casual or anonymous sex), for instance, Giddens resists equating it simply with narcissism and commitment-phobia. Set in the familiar Giddensian social landscape of detraditionalization and self-reflexivity, then, the transformation of intimacy is to be achieved through processes of questioning (most notably self-questioning), experimentation and openness.

Beck and Beck-Gernsheim similarly place individualization centrestage in their analysis, stressing the incompatibilities between self-centred biographies and codependent relationships. Unlike Giddens, however, their text is relentlessly heterosexualized (they casually brush aside 'homosexual clubs' (p. 151) in a short list of 'new roles' for men in society), and its gestures towards new forms of relationship remain firmly rooted in the heterosexual couple-form. Their list of strategies to navigate the stormy seas of love is surprisingly narrow, despite their insistence to the contrary: 'The repertoire of possibilities is broad, from premarital therapy . . ., to drawing up marriage contracts . . ., to living with someone outside marriage', to parenthood as a surrogate source of and outlet for love (p. 72). Reflexivity, then, weakens the bonds of love for Beck and Beck-Gersheim, and the future bodes ill as love becomes 'rationalized': 'What we shall have [in the future] is a social hybrid of market forces and personal impulses, an ideal of love (or marriage or parenthood) which is safe, calculable and medically optimized' (p. 141). Reforms in welfare and work – not reforms in romance – are held up as ways to save love from its destruction as individuals build up 'market biographies' that have little room for love; resisting (at least in name) the easy role-model of the nuclear family, Beck and Beck-Gernsheim search instead for a 'post-bourgeois' or 'post-familial' family, for 'new ways to live separately together' (p. 164; see also Beck-Gernsheim, 1999). Their recognition of the twin impulses inherent in detraditionalized, non-religious and individualized late-modern life – that the family is simultaneously disintegrating and being put on a pedestal – leads to the (gloomy or cosy, depending on your standpoint) conclusion that new ways of living and loving won't be radically different, in fact, from those we know now: Katherine O'Donovan (1993) refers to this as the 'uniform monotony' of love-fates. True, there are hints of Giddens' confluent love to be found in Beck and Beck-Gernsheim's rewrite, for example in their (similarly power-blind) declaration that 'no one except the lovers can decide whether they are in love – a radical form of democracy for two' (p. 192), but their sense of experimentation is a somewhat muted one. Most notably, Beck and Beck-Gernsheim give little room to considerations of nonmonogamy, polyamory or 'episodic sexuality' as ways to move love beyond the constraints of the couple – a conservatism that separates their love-view from Giddens' manifesto for negotiated, reflexive, consensual pluralism. We'd like to stay with monogamy and nonmonogamy a little longer, in order to consider arguments that infidelity has a critical – and political – function in undermining the logics of love.

Citizenship and fidelity

If we are to consider the links between intimacy and citizenship, then marriage seems a powerful place to start. As Kipnis (1998, p. 294) convincingly argues, 'marriage is meant to function as a bootcamp of citizenship instruction', meaning that its transgression via adultery can be construed as an act of bad citizenship. Adultery is, therefore, an unthinkable act not just against the partner, but against the nation:

> sex with someone who isn't your spouse means betraying the state as well as your mate... In the nation of marriage, adultery is traitorship... Infidelity makes you an infidel to the law, for which your spouse becomes an emblem, the hinge between the privacy of your desires and the power of the state installed right there in your master bedroom. (p. 300)

Interpersonal fidelity, then, becomes writ large at the level of the nation, since the ideological work done by marriage underpins the social relations of national citizenship. Arguing for a position out-side this framework, as Kipnis illustrates, is a tough call: given the way it gets explained away as either foolishness or compulsion, where can adultery find a foothold? Kipnis urges that such a foot-hold *must* be found, through the carving out of 'experimental spaces' (such as the space of adultery), which can then shed critical light on taken-for-granted social structures – a counterpublic of adultery. This is the power of adultery-as-critique: that it reveals the fragility of all contracts and vows, including those of citizenship, and that it offers transgressive pleasure through 'profaning' the institution of the couple. Kipnis (p. 322) paints from here a heady picture of the 'adulterous avant-gardes' and their intimacy-work: 'In adultery, the most conventional people in the world suddenly experience emotional free fall: unbounded intimacy outside con-tracts, law, and property relations. . . . Propelled into relations of nonidentity with dominant social forms, you're suddenly out of alignment with the reality principle and the social administration of desire. A "stray." '

Kipnis recognizes the utopian tone of this argument, and makes a convincing case for the value of such utopianism in the wake of social structures and norms that would seek to exclude such experi-mentation, or consign it to psychological and/or moral imbalance. We are reminded here of Foucault's insistence on the destabilizing effects of playfulness – of *straying* – in matters of intimacy (see also Miller, 1993). A similar attempt to work through the potency of both fidelity and adultery is to be found in Adam Phillips' *Mono-gamy* (1996). Phillips attempts to locate intimate arrangements within a personal-political framework that has some resonances with Kipnis (and with Giddens): for instance, in his declaration that 'Because erotic life rearranges the world it is political' (p. 72) and in his heroizing of adulterers.

What is particularly useful about the critical purchase of adultery is its recognition that to fight for change in the intimate sphere, we have to call on tactics that do not seek to turn away from love completely. Indeed, as Jackie Stacey and Lynne Pearce (1995) point out, transforming intimacy becomes the only strategy worth con-sidering, since attempts to jettison or refuse it totally are unlikely to work. Why is this? Stacey and Pearce argue convincingly that romance has already transformed, but that it nevertheless remains one of the central discourses of modern selfhood and society. As they sum the position up, '[w]e may (as individuals, as communities, as nations) no longer *believe* in love, but we still fall for it' (p. 12). In 'postmodern romance', Stacey and Pearce suggest, the pleasures of love can be combined with a critical irony – a position that, again, seems to bear echoes of Giddens' confluent, contingent, reflexive love. Phillips' aphorisms on monogamy also bear the inscription of this irony, as does Kipnis' championing of adultery as a mode of confluent loving.

Such a stance seems more productive, ultimately, than work which seeks to dismiss love totally, without offering anything in its place. Nicola Field (1995, p. 30), for example, does not mince her words in condemning love, writing that 'romance, far from being a fluffy, harmless, heart-shaped cushion on which lovers dally is actually an ideological weapon which serves to regulate, sweeten and pacify'. However, we do not want to cast Field's analysis aside completely, though we would want to offer a more nuanced take that can critique romance as ideological while simultaneously retaining some of its counterideological potential. What is useful in Field's account is her movement outwards from the interpersonal to consider patriotism as a form of romance – which is obviously important for thinking about citizenship – and her discussion of certain aspects of the 'gay community', such as coming-out and discourses of 'gay sensibility', as tinged with romanticism:

> Gay romanticism is about specialness, an identity based on being victimised, being oppressed and marginalised, ennobled through suffering.... Gay sensibility is about having felt the pangs of forbidden love and the fear of isolation and then moved into a new consciousness of pride, of membership of a community of one's 'own kind'.... This concept of separateness has a two-fold political repercussion. First, it means that there is a clear-cut gay market demarcation... Second, it has led to a straitening and reduction of the vision of gay liberation into a lukewarm set of meagre single-issue demands which reflect the very few common interests of a fictional cross-class 'community'. (p. 37)

There is a lot to unpack in this quite complex set of points, and we attend to some of it elsewhere. Her suggestion that oppression gets romanticized in 'gay sensibility' obviously erases the (profoundly unromantic) material experiences of marginalization – although we find useful echoes here of Susan Bickford's (1997) arguments about the political impotency of *ressentiment* (an obsession with victimhood levered by 'righteous victims'; see also Brown, 1995). But Field is right to point out the watering-down of gay liberation; the fact that one of those single-issue demands made by the 'gay community' is the right to marriage is especially problematic (see also chapter 3). Where the Gay Liberation Front had once called for shaking heteronormative society to its very foundations, campaigners now settle for fitting into (and aping) dominant modes of living – from 'Smash the Family' to 'Families We Choose', as Cindy Patton (1999) puts it. We should be mindful, though, that a similiar tinge of romanticism slides into accounts of gay liberation (which certainly inflects Field's writing) – a kind of *anti-romantic romanticism* that harks back to more radical days and agendas.

Moreover, *contra* Field's dismissal of the gay community as nothing more than a market niche, we have to recognize the importance of the community as a space of relationships. Indeed, the link between interpersonal relationships and community-building has to be seen as a central part of homosexual politics, as Jeffrey Weeks pointed out during his GLF days, in *Coming Out*: 'To build relationships is thus still a political act for homosexuals: to establish links and ties – on various levels – which transcend the yawning chasms between people' (1977, p. 236). Obviously in the decades since Weeks first wrote *Coming Out*, things have changed considerably (note that for the second edition of his book, published in 1990, Weeks jettisoned the final chapter – from which this quote comes – on the grounds that things have changed, negating the (utopian socialist) future of lesbian and gay politics he called for in 1977). The 'gay community' *has* been colonized by capital, as we have already seen; agendas have been and are being reshaped (as, indeed, they have to be). Nevertheless, we have to look at the historical and contemporary importance of the space of 'community' for the solidification of homosexual politics and identity – and, in the context of this chapter, the role played by the 'gay community' in fostering new modes of relationship where love, sex and friendship could (and can) be rearticulated away from the normative, dyadic, exclusive couple-form.

The sexual politics of friendship

Michel Foucault (1989b, p. 225) famously referred to New York and San Francisco's bath-houses and public-sex spaces as 'laboratories of sexual experimentation'. We would like to suggest that such places are also *laboratories of love and friendship* – for, as Foucault elaborates, there is much more than sex occurring in such zones. In 'Friendship as a way of life' (1989a, p. 207), he describes (male) homosexuality as 'an historic occasion to re-open affective and relational virtualities, not so much through the intrinsic qualities of the homosexual, but due to the biases against the position he occupies; in a certain sense diagonal lines that he can trace in the social fabric permit him to make these virtualities possible'. And, earlier in the interview, he poses a rhetorical question, and then suggests some answers to it:

> 'What relations, through homosexuality, can be established, invented, multiplied and modulated?' The problem is not to discover in oneself the truth of sex but rather to use sexuality henceforth to arrive at a multiplicity of relationships. . . . I think that's what makes homosexuality 'disturbing': the homosexual mode of life much more than the sexual act itself. . . . We must escape and help others escape the two ready-made formulas of the pure sexual encounter and the lovers' fusion of identities.   (pp. 204–6)

In another interview tracing some of these ideas, Foucault (1997) argues that a history of friendships must be written, partly to uncover the disappearance of friendship as the flipside to the appearance of the homosexual. Rediscovering friendship thus becomes central to homosexual politics. Sue Golding's essay 'Pariah bodies', which includes material written for photographer Tessa Boffin's funeral, echoes Foucault's call to rethink love and friendship:

> It's time we try, once again, to re-remember – not just how to love – but that we *must* love in the fullest sense of the word Respect for all the mutating, unchartable and unbearable differences each of us have within us. Is this not precisely, at least in part, what it means to be gay in all its damnable, gossipy, campy and heartbreaking ways?   (1995, p. 177)

For Foucault, as for Golding, then, friendship and love are central to the *difference* of homosexuality; ways of relating to one another that transcend the 'ready-made formulas' of heteronormative intimacy, tracing the diagonal lines of difference that can make new virtualities possible. As Lauren Berlant and Michael Warner (1998, p. 558) write: '[m]aking a queer world has required the development of kinds of intimacy that bear no necessary relation to domestic space, to kinship, to the couple form, to property, or to the nation' – making them, in the eyes of 'good folks', 'criminal intimacies' (note their use of the word *necessary*; as we shall see, some of the emerging forms of counterintimacy still bear relation to those sites that Berlant and Warner reel off). Indeed, Henning Bech (1997) suggests that one of the great social innovations of gay culture is to have separated love, sex and friendship, arguing that the categories 'friend', 'lover', 'partner' (and others) exist in fluidity, sometimes coming together (when friends are also sexual partners), but equally tenable in disconnection. Sex need not be framed by love, love need not mean sexual fidelity, and so on – relationships become rhizomatic. Bech later lists some of the more prominent forms of gay-male relationship in a passage that, although it is by no means exhaustive, makes Beck and Beck-Gernsheim's 'repertoire of possibilities' for the heterosexual couple seem hopelessly unimaginative and limited:

> there are traditions of many different ways of life in the homosexual world: apart from long-term monogamous couples, there are e.g. serial monogamies; couples with institutionalized infidelity; marriages of convenience; organized *ménage-à-trois* set-ups; close, steady, non-sexual two-person friendships; ways of life that centre on the social life of organizations, friendship networks or pub environments; intense intercourse with pornography; and combinations of these. (Bech, 1997, p. 147)

As Foucault and Bech both suggest, the lack of any pregiven relationship forms meant that the emerging affective 'homosexual culture' lacked any social scripts to live by, affording a sense of freedom. This freedom is part of what makes gay friendship *political*. Indeed, we might broaden this assertion out to consider the political force of friendship more generally; as Little (1989, quoted in Nardi,

1992, p. 116) writes, 'progress in democracy depends on a new generation that will increasingly locate itself in identity-shaping, social, yet personally liberating, friendships'. And Jacques Derrida suggests, in his *Politics of Friendship* (1997), that western democracy has always been modelled on a certain conception of friendship; new models of friendship therefore hold the promise of new models of democracy, and what we might call the *sexual politics of friendship*, then, calls for a remaking of sexual citizenship.

Tracking the (white, middle-class) American history of gay male culture, Steven Seidman (1991) locates in the 1960s and 1970s the creation of an 'indigenous cultural apparatus', centred on the emerging gay press, as fundamental to providing some sense of scripting, to fill the gap for new models of relationship – but with scripts that were gay-defined, facilitating forms of play and experimentation, and a new culture of intimacy. Seidman's discussion of the social complexity of 'casual sex' in 1970s gay-male culture, which is more nuanced than Giddens', recognizes its role within the dense web of relationships, describing an *ethics of casual sex* that includes affection, care, respect, consent and playfulness. Seidman also chides gay assimilationists for pathologizing and infantalizing casual sex and for uncritically endorsing a model of relationships based on monogamous marriage instead – what he refers to as a 'romantic sexual ethic' (p. 187). Importantly, Seidman places casual sex at the centre of developments towards a 'gay community' in 1970s America, conferring upon it a libertarian and 'communitarian' role, and crediting it with precipitating new patterns of kinship. This function has, critics argue, been too easily forgotten in the rush towards assimilationism and the formulation of the model of the 'good homosexual citizen' in 1990s gay culture: 'Respectable gays like to think that they owe nothing to the sexual subculture they think of as sleazy. But their success, their way of living, their political rights, and their very identities would never have been possible but for the existence of the public sexual culture they now despise' (Berlant and Warner, 1998, p. 563).

The resurgence of the romantic sexual ethic in the wake of AIDS, Seidman argues, has muted this libertarian, sex-positive attitude, replacing it with a culture of purity and restraint that views sex as necessarily and exclusively tied to intimacy and romance; 're-inventing monogamy', as Laura Kipnis (1998, p. 308) puts it, 'under the guise of heathful living and a new, greener terminology of renunciation: "sexual ecology"' (see also Patton, 1999). Seidman traces the emergence of such purity discourses in contemporary American (heterosexual) sex manuals, which seek to 'respiritualize' love and sex, recementing the links between the two within a national intimate culture that places marriage as not only the most fulfilling but also the only legitimate relationship form.

Family love

The attraction of the re-assertion of traditional values concerning family and sexual life is that it offers a symbolic focus for the resolution of personal and social problems that might otherwise seem intractable.   (Weeks, 1991, p. 143)

One of the central ways in which such a recementing has taken place is via the discourse of the family as the *necessary* site for intimate citizenship. As Berlant and Warner (1998, p. 550) note, '[t]he nostalgic family values covenant of contemporary American politics stipulates a privatization of citizenship and sex', mobilized through state apparatuses such as welfare, taxation, education and (as seen in New York City) through property zoning seeking to displace sites of 'public sex' (Dangerous Bedfellows, 1996). And an almost identical discourse of familialism has been central to both new right and centre-left politics in the UK, too (for example, Cooper and Herman, 1995; Stacey, 1998). Heteronormativity, as the dominant bearer of such ideologies, is produced through these discourses as a marker of citizenship, penetrating individual and collective life in ways far removed from sexual and romantic practice. Berlant and Warner (1998, p. 555) produce a dizzying list of such everyday sites of familial heteronormativity: 'paying taxes, being disgusted, philandering, bequeathing, celebrating a holiday, investing for the future, teaching, disposing of a corpse, carrying wallet photos, buying economy size, being nepotistic, running for president, divorcing, or owning anything "His" and "Hers"'.

The family is, as we have already seen, the primary *moral* location where sexual citizenship is affirmed; families are assumed to be a good thing almost by definition. Jo Van Every (1992, p. 74) argues persuasively that '[m]ost people see "family" as a good thing precisely because they consider it to be about emotional relationships. It is not considered to be an economic contract or an oppressive institution.' However, the family is more than ever being seen as attractive by lesbians and gay men, many of whom would count themselves as hostile towards the kind of queer forms of alternative intimate citizenship discussed earlier. A much more critical awareness of the limitations of coupledom is necessary, then, to correct the hegemony of romantic love as the cornerstone of lesbian and gay sexualities. Those rushing to advocate the desirability of domestic partnerships or gay marriage often do so uncritically. They reinforce the ideological role of romantic love, which then undermines diversity in living arrangements, while all the time reinforcing a conservative and assimilationist agenda, as we saw in chapter 3.

As with love and romance, many contemporary critical stances have often sought to find a way of *negotiating* rather than negating the discourse of the family, shifting its register through notions such as 'families we choose' – although outright negations do exist in contemporary literature, as in Field's *Over the Rainbow* (1995). By contrast, Kath Weston's ethnography of Bay Area 'gay families' stresses the creativity of such reconstructions of kinship among networks of friends, which frequently centre love as the defining criterion of 'family' membership:

> Grounding kinship in love deemphasised distinctions between erotic and non-erotic relations while bringing friends, lovers, and children together under a single concept. As such, love offered a symbol well suited to carry the nuances of identity and unity so central to kinship in the United States, yet circumvent the procreative assumption embedded in symbols like heterosexual intercourse and blood ties. (1998, p. 392)

Kinship, then, becomes a matter of consensual or shared identification, as well as a matter of choice, although Weston also notes that the lack of institutionalized rituals and definitions was sometimes problematic for those people she talked to (though equally, respondents described this as exciting). She locates the emergence of 'gay families' as an outcome of the historical development of gay friendship and community; particularly important for Weston in this context is the blurring of boundaries between (non-erotic) friendship and (erotic) partnership, which effectively opened up space for a notion of the family bridging the erotic and the non-erotic, bringing lovers together with friends. Of course, we find ourselves once more faced with having to address the issues raised by this building of families of choice, since, like gay marriage, there is an inevitable trace of assimilationism in the desire to make over the family.

Greg Woods' survey of gay male literature points to two currents in gay culture's imaginings of the family: the creation of '*alternative families*' and the creation of '*alternatives to the family*' (1998, p. 345, our emphasis). The difference between the two might seem slight, but it raises the question of strategies that confront the cultural politics of the family in very different ways. Of course, as Woods says, radical challenges are posed by both strategies – as the Thatcher administration's attack on 'pretended families' in Section 28 clearly shows, making new families can be seen as threatening to heteronormativity, which is given the only legitimized right of family formation. But this argument has the same ring to it as that surrounding gay marriage (that the product may be mainstream while the project is radical). And while, as Weston's research clearly demonstrates, 'families we choose' can be radically different from 'traditional' families, does their very existence testify to the power of familial ideology itself, effectively legitimating (even romanticizing) the family as a 'natural' institution? Jeffrey Weeks (1991, p. 150) puts it thus: 'the broadening of the term "family"...takes for granted the discourse of family life, and simply incorporates every other form of workable life-style into it'. Further, does the inability to create and sustain legitimated alternatives to the family (communes, for example) add more weight to this view of certain forms of family as 'natural' and others as 'unnatural'? Weeks (1997, p. 322) points out quite rightly that '[s]o many of these phenomena [e.g. 'gay families'] are extremely ambivalent. They can have a radical moment and a conservative moment' – the question perhaps then becomes how (and by whom) this distinction is mobilized. In *The Queen of America Goes to Washington City*, Lauren Berlant (1997, p. 9) offers a cautionary note on this matter, which we would like to underline: 'a politics that advocates the subaltern appropriation of normative forms of the good life makes a kind of (often tacit) peace with exploitation and normativity'. There is a strong sense, despite insistences that 'families we choose' are not surrogates but radical departures, that buying into the ideology of the family as the organizing logic of intimate and social life has to be seen in that way: as a wish for a kind of normalcy.

Counterintimacies

Against such an impulse for normalcy, Berlant and Warner (1998) situate queer culture as necessarily oppositional, as having to work outside such a normalizing framework – forging what they name 'border intimacies' or 'counterintimacies'.[1] They also highlight the ways in which AIDS has led to certain kinds of reconfiguration not just of the erotic, but of questions of friendship, love and family, as well as of the politics of these. Jeffrey Weeks and Sue Golding's conversation, in *The Eight Technologies of Otherness* (Weeks, 1997), likewise turns to the impacts of AIDS on the politics of friendship: while Golding keenly articulates her anger, and her notion of friendship-as-anger (or anger-as-friendship) as a response to AIDS, Weeks seeks to turn it into love – talking of love as the only way to live in the face of death (see also Weeks, 1995). Now, we could locate this difference in a kind of intergenerational way – Golding's anger as a *queer* response versus Weeks' post-gay-lib sensibilities (we are reminded of John D'Emilio's (1992, p. 220) admonition, in an essay on AIDS, that 'you can't build a movement on anger'. He goes even further, arguing that any emotional response be removed from political action, which should be based on *thinking* rather than *feeling*.) But it seems that the anger/love dichotomy set up is a false one: isn't anger *part of* love? The rage that Golding writes out in many of her essays is born out of her sense of connectivity, of friendship, of love. Weeks and D'Emilio both seek to sideline anger's politics; however, Susan Bickford (1997) makes a much more fruitful case for reassessing anger as one of her 'passions of citizenship'. Drawing on the work of Audre Lorde, Bickford discusses 'creative' *political* uses of anger:

> Anger is energy directed toward another in an attempt to create a relationship between subjects that is not 'distorted' (made unjust) by

hierarchies of power and the way subjects work within those hierarchies. If those hierarchies are to be changed through political
interaction, then recreating the relationship between subjects is a
central step. To recognize anger as a possible force in that reconstruction is to recognize the specificity of the creatures who engage
with one another; it neither requires us to deny ourselves nor prevents our connecting with others.　(p. 125)

Anger is, then, a 'public passion' of citizenship which must not be
purged from politics (*contra* D'Emilio); instead, as Bickford suggests,
we should seek to find ways of using anger politically. The anger of
AIDS activists has to be seen in this context; to deny the political
force of that anger, as John D'Emilio would like us to, is to diminish
the efforts of dissident citizens to fight for justice.

AIDS has, of course, had a profoundly reorienting effect on concepts of intimacy, caring, the erotic and love, as many commentators have described (e.g. Singer, 1993). Barry Adam (1992), for
example, discusses the ways in which AIDS organizations draw
upon and extend models of friendship networks among gay men,
creating 'care relationships' to respond to the crisis (such as buddying) – although he also points to the experiences of bureaucratization and clientization with the AIDS-care system that move it away
from friendship. Also of central importance has been the symboliz-
ing of this care and love (and anger), through, for instance, the
displaying of AIDS quilts and the holding of vigils (see also Brown,
1997). As Weeks (1995) paradoxically suggests, the ethic of care
brought about by AIDS revolves around values normally lodged in
the notion of family life – although how that might be squared with
the *realities* of family life for those living with HIV/AIDS is an issue
he fails to consider. He goes on to argue, instead, that 'AIDS
provides a reflector through which we can witness the uncertainties of our attitudes to life, love and death – but also the possibilities
which are giving them new meanings' (p. 159).

This leads Weeks on to devising a new 'alternative ethics of love'
comprising care, responsibility, respect and knowledge (axes bor-
rowed and reworked from Erich Fromm's *The Art of Loving* (1957)).
The four dimensions of this love ethic are knitted together by Weeks
to form 'a sense of the indissoluble link between the individual and
the social, and...the personal and the political' (1995, p. 185),

which takes us right back to Giddens' claim that sorting out intimacy is the way to sort out democracy. In fact, Weeks is not alone in finding love at the end of thinking about sexual politics; in *Getting Specific* (1994), Shane Phelan similarly summons up love as a commitment to the welfare of others, which, importantly for her, does not rely upon sameness (in the way that other forms of identitarian commitment often can). And, reflecting on Phelan's imperative, Sally Munt (1998, p. 18) demands that we 'deromanticize love', making it over as an ethics of care; love is, she writes, a 'heroic desire that acknowledges and includes our commonalities and our differences without homogenizing conflict... and [that] embraces the specifics of people's real material needs'. Arguing in the opposite direction, however, Cindy Patton (1999, p. 370) confesses that she 'can't quite bring myself to formulate or advocate a new politics of love.... [L]ove is too dangerous a basis for social politics' in response to the AIDS crisis, since the new politics of love asserts a community-based ethic of care in place of the bond made by sex.

What these calls to love all share, in their different ways, is an acknowledgement of the need to reformulate what love means – for Munt this entails love's deromanticization, while for Giddens our conception of intimacy must be rewritten away from the (similarly romantic) scripts of long-term monogamous heterosexuality (taking us towards 'confluent love' and 'pure relationships'). Being proscriptive about new modes of loving is clearly a difficult task, as evidenced by the often vague ways it is discussed by theorists. Perhaps this illustrates the discursive power of hegemonic scripts of love – that, as Kipnis and Berlant and Warner have all suggested, imagining intimacy anew calls for flights of fancy. But this remains a vital task: by creating what Michel Foucault (1989b, p. 229) called 'as yet unforeseen kinds of relationships' – which can begin to rework what we mean by love, what we mean by family, what we mean by friendship – we might be able to rethink from here what we mean by citizenship; or, perhaps, what we mean by *as yet unforeseen kinds of citizenship*.

9

Hard Choices

What we hope to have achieved through the preceding eight chapters of this book is the mapping of some key domains of sexual citizenship. As we said at the outset, we want to make clear that the figure of the sexual citizen is an ambivalent one; certainly, the strategies deployed in the project of sexual citizenship are marked by ambivalence. This is summed up in the tension between the titles of two books on the theme, Andrew Sullivan's assimilationist manifesto *Virtually Normal* (1996) and Michael Warner's queer response to assimilationism, *The Trouble With Normal* (1999). In one sense, that's what the hard choices facing the sexual citizen are: the push towards rights claims that make dissident sexualities fit into heterosexual culture, by demanding equality and recognition, versus the demand to reject settling for heteronormativity through, for example, sex-positive strategies of refusal – the kind of practices and identities enacted in queer counterpublics.

It should be obvious that things aren't that simple, however – they never are. By moving through different domains of sexual citizenship, we have attempted to locate and contextualize ways of figuring the sexual citizen in relation to particular issues and modes of politics. In our view, we cannot simply decide to side with Sullivan or Warner, but have to consider the specific implications of strategies. For example, our discussion of debates on marriage and military service require that we disentangle the issues raised; we agree with Claudia Card (1996) that we shouldn't necessarily read both imperatives in the same way. By thinking about class, for instance, we can read the two debates as having potentially very different outcomes.

That kind of approach, then, has informed our analysis in each chapter. We established early on that we need to see citizenship as a sexualized project, meaning that everyone is a sexual citizen. However, the ways in which different sexual identities fit in with the logics of citizenship require that we attend to the intersection of discourses of citizenship with discourses of sexuality. We may all be sexual citizens, but we are not *equal* sexual citizens. That notion, of inequality in citizenship status, has come increasingly to inform sexual politics, as sexual politics itself moves towards making rights claims in the interlocking fields of law and politics. This move itself is revealing of the way that citizenship discourse has interpellated sexual dissidents as citizens – or at least as *potential* citizens. In some cases, this is a liberating moment, in that the platform of rights claims can deliver certain kinds of sexual rights by appealing to the logic of citizenship. At the same time, however, we have to remember that the fundamental articulation of citizenship matches rights with responsibilities – and we need to be mindful of the responsibilities that sexual dissidents are made to carry in the trade-off for rights.

Equally, we need to scrutinize the kinds of rights that citizenship discourse makes claimable. Again, the right to marry shows us this vividly. Claiming the right to something that has hitherto been denied to you does not justify that claim. We have to ask what rights we might want to claim, and then look for possibilities for making such claims. Or, as a growing number of critics suggest, we have to radically rethink the project of rights claims itself; if we are to concede that citizenship discourse can accommodate only a certain articulation of sexual rights, would we not be better served by refusing that agenda altogether, and finding more imaginative ways to mobilize sexual politics? This does not mean that we should not engage with citizenship, of course. As Diane Richardson (1998) clearly shows us, we can use the notion of citizenship as a powerful critical tool – to show the manifold forms of discrimination that face sexual dissidents. But that does not necessarily propel us to shape an oppositional politics from within the same frame.

Of course, that was one of the most powerful features of queer politics; that it mobilized new ways of being political. While some commentators are critical of queer politics' emphasis on transgression as a political tactic, others more keenly stress the transformative effect that queer politics has had. That's why we should be clear about the subtitle of *The Sexual Citizen*. 'Queer Politics and Beyond' should not be misrecognized as a call to move away from the queer agenda. In the same way that the term 'postfeminism' should not be misrecognized as signposting the 'end of feminism' but rather as a critical reorientation of feminist theory and politics (Barrett, 2000), we in no way mean to signal the death of queer politics. Instead, we want to point towards the negotiations and transformations in sexual politics – some of these are anti-queer, to be sure, but others maintain a commitment to queer theory and politics – which have complexified the political projects of sexual dissidence. The increasing focus on the notion of sexual citizenship is absolutely central to that transformation.

As we have already seen, for some writers a notion like 'queer citizenship' would be oxymoronic: for Jeffrey Weeks (1995, 1999), for instance, transgressive politics like queer have an important function, but this is transitory and particular, and has to be superseded by the 'moment of citizenship'. In this kind of formulation, 'queer' is the opposite of 'citizen'; this kind of dualism immediately summons up the split between 'good' and 'bad' citizens. Being a good sexual citizen can never be a queer strategy, even if the queer 'moment of transgression' might open up the space that makes the sexual citizen a possible identity to mobilize in the first place. Part of the project of sexual citizenship, then, might be to broaden and open up our conception of the citizen – in the way that someone like Holloway Sparks (1997) suggests, so that dissent and dissidence need not be considered inappropriate stances for citizens to take.

At the level of theory, such work is indeed taking place. We have seen how definitions of citizenship have expanded: for example, in taking on board the notion of cultural citizenship (Isin and Wood, 1999). But at the level of practice, of politics and of common sense, the notion of citizenship remains overdetermined by its new right origins. Political shifts towards the centre-left have failed to reshape citizenship substantially at this level. What this inevitably means for the rights-based sexual citizenship agenda is *compromise*. If, as

Carl Stychin (1998) concludes, sexual politics will continue to be articulated in terms of rights, the question becomes one of *how we use rights*. As we saw in the case of same-sex marriage, we have to ask whether rights should be claimed simply because they are currently denied. And we need to look at what might be lost when particular rights are won; importantly in this context, we have to ask *who* loses and who wins in rights claims. As we have shown throughout this book, there is often a class dimension to be considered here. Yet it seems that the mutually constitutive politics of class and sexuality have become unshackled in the current articulations of rights claims. We would want to emphasize, therefore, that our interventions into sexual citizenship must be attuned to the impact that class has on the potential to benefit from rights claims.

As we showed in our discussions of the city as a space of sexual citizenship and of the space of the social, for instance, class-based exclusions are a vector of the unevenness of access to the enabling possibilities of aspects of sexual citizenship. This is, perhaps, most apparent in discussions of consumer citizenship. Given the increasing marketization of rights, we have to recognize that the utopian promise of the pink economy is a myth which hides economic inequality. There is, as we noted, an *economic geography* to sexual citizenship; it is not, to recall Judith Butler (1997b), *merely cultural*. Reinstating class into these debates has to be seen as imperative if we are to avoid replacing discrimination based on sexuality with discrimination based on class. This is certainly a key concern for our question about who rights claims work for.

While such an imperative does not necessarily return us to queer politics – especially given critiques of queer's failure to address class adequately (Morton, 1996) – it should not urge us to embrace assimilationism either. In the USA, it has been remarked upon that the rights claims coming from the lesbian and gay movement have increasingly been oriented to securing the rights of middle-class white citizens. Queer politics, by comparison, avoids such a closed-down notion of sexual citizenship. In the context of debates over public sex, for example, the collusion of gay groups with law and politics to clean up cities sidelines those parts of dissident sexual culture least amenable to capital colonization. As the Dangerous Bedfellows Collective (1996) shows time and time again, these moves are all about economics. The erosion of queer counterpublics has to be seen to have a class dimension to it, as does the increasing focus on and celebration of visible consumption spaces in cities – so-called gay villages – as well as the growth of gentrified 'gay neighbourhoods'. Remember Allan Bérubé's (1996) recollection of coming to San Francisco and finding himself excluded from the 'great gay life' that the city promised him (or at least that his imagining of it did).

As we showed in chapter 7, another of the prominent reimaginings of citizenship – this one brought about by globalization – must similarly be read as economically structured. Just as Bérubé found that moving to San Francisco didn't allow him to live out his dream because he was too poor, so the myth of global gay identity and transnational queer space does a serious injustice to the material realities associated with mobility and the impacts of the worldwide economy. While there is indeed a privileged group of cosmopolitan sexual citizens circling the globe, there are also those who are forced to move and those who simply cannot move. As we argued in that chapter and chapter 5, in this context we need to think more carefully about the processes of globalization and their outcomes in shaping, for example, so-called global cities. As Isin and Wood (1999, p. 160) conclude, 'global cities have become a battleground in which various groups either raise rights-claims or are denied [the] ability to raise such claims'. Transnational sexual citizenship *can* work productively – for example, in the context of the internationalization of human rights law – but we have to remember that the nation-state remains for many dissident sexual citizens their primary space of experience.

A recurrent theme throughout this book has been the relationship between discourses of citizenship and those of the family. As we have seen, the family has such an ideological weight attached to it that dissident sexual citizens are increasingly attempting to find ways to make space for themselves in the family – by using notions such as 'families we choose' to broaden existing conceptualizations of what families look like. Our discussions of love and marriage have shown how these attempts to change the meaning of family have superseded previous stances in sexual politics, which sought to reject the family as inherently heteronormative. The trouble with family, as we have seen, is that it is a term with too many things attached to it; it is too embedded in ideas about love, sex, relation-ships, privacy, ownership, responsibility and so on. Trying to revolu-tionize the family, by pluralizing it to 'families', and coining terms like 'alternative families', has become the dominant response to the enduring centrality of family within sexual citizenship (Patton, 1999). The problem with families we choose is that not everyone can choose what kind of family they are in (or not in). The much-vaunted democratization of relationships, the arrival of the post-familial family (Beck-Gernsheim, 1999), again denies material realities for too many people unable to engage in experimental modes of relationship. In addition, the continuing relationship between the couple-form, the family and crucial aspects of citizen-ship like welfare provision serves to cement aspects of social exclu-sion for those attempting to resist becoming familial citizens (Probyn, 1998).

All of this brings us back to the hard choices the sexual citizen is currently faced with. It should be more than clear by now, as we come to the end of our discussions, that finding ways to be a sexual citizen will inevitably involve having to face those choices. Choos-ing how to articulate sexual citizenship in ways that work for us all is an enormous task; but it is a task that we cannot ignore, for it seems that the choice to disidentify – to remain as non-citizens – will maintain systems of exclusion and discrimination that bring real material harm to many people. But we should always keep a critical eye on the moves we make to secure status as citizens, and look around at the potential harm any rights claims might have on others. A critical, contextualized approach to the different domains of sexual citizenship is thus essential; we hope to have contributed to that process here.

Notes

Chapter 3 Marriage, the Military and the Sexual Citizen

1   In her provocative essay 'Adultery' (to which we devote more atten-
    tion in chapter 8), Laura Kipnis (1997, p. 320) notes an analogous
    argument from Slavoj Žižek, who suggests that 'the Law secretly
    condones transgression, . . . making the only true transgression pub-
    licly overidentifying with its dictates'. Such a tactic may also be found
    in the work of Decadent Action, who seek to destroy capitalism
    through a dedicated programme of overindulgence and conspicuous
    consumption (Decadent Action, 1997). It might be possible, then, to
    argue that the fight for lesbian and gay marriage operates in the way
    Žižek describes; we remain, however, less than fully convinced by this,
    especially in the light of the kinds of argument forwarded by most
    advocates of same-sex partnership registration, which stress assimila-
    tion and normalcy.

Chapter 7 Transnational Sexual Citizenship

1   Lisa Grant, denied employee benefits for her lesbian partner, and the
    group of men convicted for consensual same-sex sadomasochism in
    the wake of Operation Spanner both took their cases to the European
    courts – and lost.

Chapter 8 Turn it into Love

1   In her essay 'Extraordinary homosexuals and the fear of being ordin-
    ary' (1994, p. 123) Biddy Martin takes a polar-opposite stance to
    Berlant and Warner, arguing that '[r]adical anti-normativity throws
    out a lot of babies with a lot of bathwater', and criticizing queer
    theorists for their 'enormous fear of ordinariness or normalcy'; how-
    ever, we find Berlant's point about the perils of a quest for ordinariness
    – and the compromises it embodies – to be the more persuasive at this
    juncture.

References

Adam, Barry 1992: Sex and caring among gay men: impacts of AIDS on gay people. In Ken Plummer (ed.), *Modern Homosexualities: fragments of lesbian and gay experience*, London: Routledge, 175–83.

Ainley, Rosa 1998: Introduction. In Rosa Ainley (ed.), *New Frontiers of Space, Bodies and Gender*, London: Routledge, xiii–xvii.

Allen, Dennis 1995: Homosexuality and narrative. *Modern Fiction Studies*, 41, 609–34.

Altman, Dennis 1996: Rupture or continuity? The internationalization of gay identities. *Social Text*, 48, 77–94.

Appadurai, Arjun 1996: *Modernity at Large: cultural dimensions of globalization*. Minneapolis: University of Minnesota Press.

Aronowitz, Stanley 1995: Against the liberal state: ACT-UP and the emergence of postmodern politics. In Linda Nicholson and Steven Seidman (eds), *Social Postmodernism: beyond identity politics*, Cambridge: Cambridge University Press, 357–83.

Barrett, Michele (2000) Post-feminism. In Gary Browning, Abigail Halcli and Frank Webster (eds), *Understanding Contemporary Society: theories of the present*, London: Sage, 46–56.

Barsky, Robert 1994: Making love with [Bakhtin]. *GLQ*, 1, 135–41.

Barthes, Roland 1973: *Mythologies*. St Albans: Paladin.

—— (1977/1990) *A Lover's Discourse: fragments*. London: Penguin.

Bawer, Bruce 1993: *A Place at the Table: the gay individual in American society*. New York: Touchstone Books.

Bech, Henning 1992: Report from a rotten state: 'marriage' and 'homosexuality' in 'Denmark'. In Ken Plummer (ed.), *Modern Homo-*

sexualities: fragments of lesbian and gay experience, London: Routledge, 134–47.

—— 1997: *When Men Meet: homosexuality and modernity*. Cambridge: Polity Press.

—— 1999: Citysex: representing lust in public. In Mike Featherstone (ed.), *Love and Eroticism*, London: Sage, 215–42.

Beck, Ulrich and Beck-Gernsheim, Elisabeth 1995: *The Normal Chaos of Love*. Cambridge: Polity Press.

Beck-Gernsheim, Elisabeth 1999: On the way to a post-familial family: from a community of need to elective affinities. In Mike Featherstone (ed.), *Love and Eroticism*, London: Sage, 53–70.

Bell, David 1995a: Perverse dynamics, sexual citizenship and the transformation of intimacy. In David Bell and Gill Valentine (eds), *Mapping Desire: geographies of sexualities*, London: Routledge, 304–17.

—— 1995b: Pleasure and danger: the paradoxical spaces of sexual citizenship. *Political Geography*, 14, 139–53.

—— 1997: Review of Davina Cooper, *Power in Struggle. Social and Legal Studies*, 6, 458–9.

—— 2000: Farm boys and wild men: rurality, masculinity, and homosexuality. *Rural Sociology*, forthcoming.

Bell, David and Binnie, Jon 1998: Theatres of cruelty, rivers of desire: the erotics of the street. In Nicholas Fyfe (ed.), *Images of the Street: planning, identity and control in public space*, London: Routledge, 129–40.

Berlant, Lauren 1997: *The Queen of America Goes to Washington City: essays on sex and citizenship*. Durham, NC: Duke University Press.

—— 1998: Intimacy: a special issue. *Critical Inquiry*, 24, 281–8.

Berlant, Lauren and Freedman, Elizabeth 1993: Queer nationality. In Michael Warner (ed.), *Fear of a Queer Planet: queer politics and social theory*, Minneapolis: University of Minnesota Press, 193–229.

Berlant, Lauren and Warner, Michael 1998: Sex in public. *Critical Inquiry*, 24, 547–66.

Bérubé, Allan 1996: Intellectual desire. *GLQ*, 3, 139–57.

Bickford, Susan 1997: Anti-anti-identity politics: feminism, democracy, and the complexities of citizenship. *Hypatia*, 12, 111–31.

Binnie, Jon 1995: Trading places: consumption, sexuality and the production of queer space. In David Bell and Gill Valentine (eds), *Mapping Desire: geographies of sexualities*, London: Routledge, 182–99.

—— 1997: Invisible Europeans: sexual citizenship in the new Europe. *Environment and Planning A*, 29, 237–48.

—— 1998: Re-stating the place of sexual citizenship. *Environment and Planning D: Society and Space*, 16, 367–9.

—— 2000: Cosmopolitanism and the sexed city. In David Bell and Azzedine Haddour (eds), *City Visions*, Harlow: Prentice-Hall, 166–78.

Binnie, Jon and Skeggs, Beverley 1999: Cosmopolitan sexualities: disrupting the logic of late capitalism? Paper presented at the Fourth International Metropolis Conference, 8–11 December, Washington, DC.

Blair, Tony 1996: *New Britain: my vision for a young country*. London: Fourth Estate.

Brennan, Timothy 1997: *At Home in the World: cosmopolitanism now*. Cambridge, MA: Harvard University Press.

Brown, Michael 1997: *RePlacing Citizenship: AIDS activism and radical democracy*. New York: Guilford.

Brown, Wendy 1995: *States of Injury: power and freedom in late modernity*. Princeton, NJ: Princeton University Press.

Brownworth, Victoria 1996: Tying the knot or the hangman's noose: the case against marriage. *Journal of Gay, Lesbian, and Bisexual Identity*, 1, 91–8.

Burkitt, Brian and Ashton, Frances 1996: The birth of the stakeholder society. *Critical Social Policy*, 49, 3–16.

Butler, Judith 1993: *Bodies that Matter: on the discursive limits of 'sex'*. New York: Routledge.

—— 1997a: *Excitable Speech: a politics of the performative*. New York: Routledge.

—— 1997b Merely cultural? *Social Text*, 52/53, 265–78.

Califia, Pat 1994: *Public Sex: the culture of radical sex*. Pittsburgh, PA: Cleis Press.

Cant, Bob 1997: Introduction. In Bob Cant (ed.), *Invented Identities? Lesbians and gay men talk about migration*, London: Cassell, 1–18.

Card, Claudia 1996: Against marriage and motherhood. *Hypatia*, 11, 1–23.

Champagne, Rosaria 1998: Queering the unconscious. *South Atlantic Quarterly*, 97, 281–96.

Chapin, Jessica 1998: Closing America's 'back door'. *GLQ*, 4, 403–22.

Chauncey, George 1996: 'Privacy could only be had in public': gay uses of the streets. In Joel Saunders (ed.), *Stud: architectures of masculinity*, New York: Princeton Architectural Press, 244–67.

Child, Russell 1993: The economic situation in the member states. In Kees Waaldijk and Andrew Chapman (eds), *Homosexuality: a European Community issue*, Dordrecht: Martinus Nijhoff, 163–78.

Chisholm, Dianne 1999: The traffic in free love and other crises: space, pace, sex and shock in the city of late modernity. *Parallax*, 5, 69–89.

Clarke, John and Newman, Janet 1997: *The Managerial State: power, politics and ideology in the remaking of social welfare*. London: Sage.

Clarke, Paul 1996: *Deep Citizenship*. London: Pluto Press.

Cohen, Jean 1999: Changing paradigms of citizenship and the exclusiveness of the demos. *International Sociology*, 14, 245–68.

Cohen, Peter 1997: 'All they needed': AIDS, consumption, and the politics of class. *Journal of the History of Sexuality*, 8, 86–115.

Cooper, Davina 1993a: An engaged state: sexuality, governance, and the potential for change. *Journal of Law and Society*, 20, 257–75.

—— 1993b: The Citizen's Charter and radical democracy: empowerment and exclusion within citizenship discourse. *Social and Legal Studies*, 2, 149–71.

—— 1994: *Sexing the City: lesbian and gay politics within the activist state*. London: Rivers Oram.

—— 1995: *Power in Struggle: feminism, sexuality and the state*. Buckingham: Open University Press.

—— 1998: Regard between strangers: diversity, equality and the reconstruction of public space. *Critical Social Policy*, 18, 465–92.

Cooper, Davina and Herman, Didi 1995: Getting 'the family right': legislating heterosexuality in Britain, 1986–91. In Didi Herman and Carl Stychin (eds), *Legal Inversions: lesbians, gay men, and the politics of law*, Philadelphia: Temple University Press, 162–79.

Crimp, Douglas 1987: How to have promiscuity in an epidemic. *October*, 43, 237–71.

Crimp, Douglas and Rolston, Adam 1990: *AIDS Demo Graphics*. Seattle, WA: Bay Press.

Currah, Paisley 1995: Searching for immutability: homosexuality, race and rights discourse. In Angelia Wilson (ed.), *A Simple Matter of Justice?: theorizing lesbian and gay politics*, London: Cassell, 91–109.

Dangerous Bedfellows (eds) (1996): *Policing Public Sex: queer politics and the future of AIDS activism*. Boston, MA: South End Press.

Decadent Action 1997: Decadent Action manifesto. In Stewart Home (ed.), *Mind Invaders: a reader in psychic warfare, cultural sabotage and semiotic terrorism*, London: Serpent's Tail, 1–3.

Deleuze, Gilles 1979: The rise of the social. Foreword to Jacques Donzolet, *The Policing of Families*, London: Hutchinson.

D'Emilio, Jon 1992: *Making Trouble: essays on gay history, politics, and the university*. New York: Routledge.

—— 1993: Capitalism and gay identity. In Henry Abelove, Michele A. Barale and David M. Halperin (eds), *The Lesbian and Gay Studies Reader*, London: Routledge, 467–76.

Derrida, Jacques 1997: *Politics of Friendship*. London: Verso.

Driver, Stephen and Martell, Luke 1997: New Labour's communitarianisms. *Critical Social Policy*, 52, 27–46.

Duggan, Lisa 1995: Queering the state. In Lisa Duggan and Nan D. Hunter, *Sex Wars: sexual dissent and political culture*, New York: Routledge, 178–93.

Duggan, Lisa and Hunter, Nan D. 1995: *Sex Wars: sexual dissent and political culture*. New York: Routledge.

Duyvendak, Jan Willem 1994: *De Verzuiling van de Homobeweging*. Amsterdam: SUA.

—— 1995: Gay subcultures between movement and market. In Hanspeter Kriesi, Ruud Koopmans, Jan Willem Duyvendak and Marco G. Giugni (eds), *New Social Movements in Western Europe: a comparative analysis*, London: UCL Press, 165–80.

—— 1996: The depoliticization of Dutch gay identity, or why Dutch gays aren't queer. In Steven Seidman (ed.), *Queer Theory/Sociology*, Oxford: Blackwell, 421–38.

Duyves, Mattias 1995: Framing preferences, framing differences: inventing Amsterdam as a gay capital. In Richard Parker and John Gagnon (eds), *Conceiving Sexuality: approaches to sex research in a postmodern world*, New York: Routledge, 51–66.

Dyer, Richard 1993: *The Matter of Images: essays on representation*. London: Routledge.

Edge, Simon 1995: *With Friends Like These: Marxism and gay politics*. London: Cassell.

—— 1997: Proudly, openly, equally gay. *New Statesman*, 18 July, 22–3.

Edginton, Beth 1998: Nation. *Screen*, 39,79–81.

Ellison, Nick 1997: Towards a new social politics: citizenship and reflexivity in late modernity. *Sociology*, 31, 697–717.

Escoffier, Jeffrey 1997: The political economy of the closet: notes towards an economic history of gay and lesbian life before Stonewall. In Amy Gluckman and Betsy Reed (eds), *Homo Economics: capitalism, community, and lesbian and gay life*, London: Routledge, 123–34.

Evans, David 1993: *Sexual Citizenship: the material construction of sexualities*. London: Routledge.

Fellows, Will 1996: *Farm Boys: lives of gay men from the rural Midwest*. Madison: University of Wisconsin Press.

Field, Nicola 1995: *Over the Rainbow: money, class and homophobia*. London: Pluto Press.

Foucault, Michel 1989a: Friendship as a way of life. In Sylvère Lotringer (ed.), *Foucault Live*, New York: Semiotext(e), 203–10.

—— 1989b: Sexual choice, sexual act. In Sylvère Lotringer (ed.), *Foucault Live*, New York: Semiotext(e), 211–32.

—— 1997: Sex, power, and the politics of identity. In Paul Rabinow (ed.), *Ethics: subjectivity and truth*, New York: The New Press, 163–73.

Fraser, Mariam 1999: Classing queer: politics in competition. *Theory, Culture & Society*, 16, 107–31.

Fraser, Nancy 1992: Rethinking the public sphere: a contribution to the critique of actually existing democracy. In Craig Calhoun (ed.), *Habermas and the Public Sphere*, Cambridge, MA: MIT Press.

——1997: Heterosexism, misrecognition, and capitalism: a response to Judith Butler. *Social Text*, 52/53, 279–94.

Freud, Sigmund 1921: *Group Psychology and the Analysis of the Ego*. In J. Strachey (trans. and ed.), *The Standard Edition of the Complete Psychological Works of Sigmund Freud*, London: Hogarth Press, vol. 18.

Fromm, Erich 1957: *The Art of Loving*. London: Allen and Unwin.

Fuss, Diana 1989: *Essentially Speaking: feminism, nature and difference*. New York: Routledge.

Gabriel, Yiannis and Lang, Tim 1995: *The Unmanageable Consumer: contemporary consumption and its fragmentations*. London: Sage.

Gamson, Joshua 1996: Must identity movements self-destruct?: a queer dilemma. In Steven Seidman (ed.), *Queer Theory/Sociology*, Oxford: Blackwell, 395–420.

Geltmaker, Ty 1997: The queer nation acts up: health care, politics, and sexual diversity in the County of Angels, 1990–92. In Gordon Brent Ingram, Anne-Marie Bouthillette and Yolanda Retter (eds), *Queers in Space: communities, public places, sites of resistance*, Seattle, WA: Bay Press, 233–74.

Giddens, Anthony 1991: *Modernity and Self-Identity: self and society in the late modern age*. Cambridge: Polity Press.

——1992: *The Transformation of Intimacy: sexuality, love and eroticism in modern societies*. Cambridge: Polity Press.

Gluckman, Amy and Reed, Betsy (eds) 1997: *Homo Economics: capitalism, community, and lesbian and gay life*. New York: Routledge.

Golding, Sue 1995: Pariah bodies. In Elizabeth Grosz and Elspeth Probyn (eds), *Sexy Bodies: the strange carnalities of feminism*, London: Routledge, 172–80.

Gopinath, Gayatri 1996: Funny boys and girls: notes on a queer South Asian planet. In Russell Leong (ed.), *Asian American Sexualities: dimensions of the gay and lesbian experience*, New York: Routledge, 119–27.

Gould, Paul 1998: The love that dares not forget its brand name. *Financial Times* (London), 7/8 March, xxii.

Gross, Larry 1993: *Contested Closets: the politics and ethics of outing*. Minneapolis: University of Minnesota Press.

Halley, Janet 1994: Sexual orientation and the politics of biology: a critique of the argument from immutability. *Stanford Law Journal*, 36, 301–66.

Hardisty, Jean and Gluckman, Amy 1997: The hoax of 'special rights': the right wing's attack on gay men and lesbians. In Amy Gluckman and Betsy Reed (eds), *Homo Economics: capitalism, community, and lesbian and gay life*, London: Routledge, 209–22.

Harper, Phillip 1997: Gay male identities, personal privacy, and relations of public exchange: notes on directions for queer critique. *Social Text*, 52/53, 5–29.

Haver, William 1996: *The Body of this Death: historicity and sociality in the time of AIDS*. Stanford, CA: Stanford University Press.

Hegarty, Peter 1997: Materializing the hypothalamus: a performative account of the 'gay brain'. *Feminism and Psychology*, 7, 355–72.

Hennessy, Rosemary 1993: Queer theory: a review of the *differences* special issue and Minique Wittig's *The Straight Mind*. *Signs*, 18, 964–73.

Herdt, Gilbert 1997: *Same Sex, Different Cultures: exploring gay and lesbian lives*. Boulder, CO: Westview.

Higgs, David (ed.) 1999: *Queer Sites: gay urban histories since 1800*. London: Routledge.

Hocquenghem, Guy 1993: *Homosexual Desire*. Durham, NC: Duke University Press.

Holliday, Ruth 1998: *Philadelphia*: AIDS, organization, representation. In John Hassard and Ruth Holliday (eds), *Organization/Representation*, London: Sage, 101–16.

Hunter, Nan 1995a: Banned in the USA: what the Hardwick ruling will mean. In Lisa Duggan and Nan Hunter (eds), *Sex Wars: sexual dissent and political culture*, New York: Routledge, 80–4.

—— 1995b: Marriage, law and gender: a feminist inquiry. In Lisa Duggan and Nan Hunter (eds), *Sex Wars: sexual dissent and political culture*, New York: Routledge, 107–22.

—— 1995c: Sexual dissent and the family: the Sharon Kowalski case. In Lisa Duggan and Nan Hunter (eds), *Sex Wars: sexual dissent and political culture*, New York: Routledge, 101–6.

Ignatieff, Michael 1991: Citizenship and moral narcissism. In Geoff Andrews (ed.), *Citizenship*, London: Lawrence and Wishart, 26–36.

Illouz, Eva 1997: *Consuming the Romantic Utopia: love and the cultural contradictions of capitalism*. Berkeley: University of California Press.

Isin, Engin and Wood, Patricia 1999: *Citizenship and Identity*. London: Sage.

Jackson, Peter (1999) An explosion of Thai identities: peripheral genders and the limits of queer theory. Paper presented at the IAASCS Second International Conference, Manchester.

Jackson, Stevi 1995: Women and heterosexual love: complicity, resistance and change. In Lynne Pearce and Jackie Stacey (eds), *Romance Revisited*, London: Lawrence and Wishart, 49–61.

Jamieson, Lynn 1999: Intimacy transformed? A critical look at the 'pure relationship'. *Sociology*, 33, 477–94.

Kader, C. and Piontek, T. 1992: Introduction. *Discourse*, 15, 5–10.

Kaplan, Morris 1997: Intimacy and equality: the question of lesbian and gay marriage. In Shane Phelan (ed.), *Playing with Fire: queer politics, queer theories*, New York: Routledge, 201–30.

Kayal, Philip 1993: *Bearing Witness: gay men's health crisis and the politics of AIDS*. Boulder, CO: Westview.

Kearns, Adrian 1992: Active citizenship and urban governance. *Transactions of the Institute of British Geographers*, 17, 20–34.

Kipnis, Laura 1998: Adultery. *Critical Inquiry*, 24, 289–327.

Kirk, Marshall and Madsen, Hunter 1989: *After the Ball: how America will conquer its fear and hatred of gays in the '90s*. New York: Doubleday.

Knopp, Lawrence 1995: Sexuality and urban space: a framework for analysis. In David Bell and Gill Valentine (eds), *Mapping Desire: geographies of sexualities*, London: Routledge, 149–63.

Kramer, Jerry-Lee 1995: Bachelor farmers and spinsters: gay and lesbian identities and communities in rural North Dakota. In David Bell and Gill Valentine (eds), *Mapping Desire: geographies of sexualities*, London: Routledge, 200–13.

Kushner, Tony 1997: Homosexual liberation: a socialism of the skin. In Amy Gluckman and Betsy Reed (eds), *Homo Economics: capitalism, community, and lesbian and gay life*, New York: Routledge, 185–92.

Leap, William (ed.) 1999: *Public Sex/Gay Space*. New York: Columbia University Press.

Lee Badget, M. V. 1997a: Beyond biased samples: challenging the myths on the economic status of lesbians and gay men. In Amy Gluckman and Betsy Reed (eds), *Homo Economics: capitalism, community, and lesbian and gay life*, London: Routledge, 65–71.

—— 1997b: A queer marketplace: books on lesbian and gay consumers, workers, and investors. *Feminist Studies*, 21, 607–32.

LeVay, Simon 1993: *The Sexual Brain*. Cambridge, MA: MIT Press.

—— 1996: *Queer Science*. Cambridge, MA: MIT Press.

Lowe, Donald M. 1995: *The Body in Late-Capitalist USA*. Durham, NC: Duke University Press.

Luibheid, Eithne 1998: 'Looking like a lesbian': the organization of sexual monitoring at the United States–Mexico border. *Journal of the History of Sexuality*, 8, 477–506.

Lyttle, John 1998: Dazzled by shiny, happy, out New Labour. *Independent*, 4 June, 5.

McGhee, Derek 1998: Looking and acting the part: gays in the armed forces – a case of passing masculinity. *Feminist Legal Studies*, 4, 205–44.

McRobbie, Angela 1997: Pecs and penises: the meaning of girlie culture. *Soundings*, 5, 157–66.

Manalansan IV, Martin F. 1995: In the shadows of Stonewall: examining gay transnational politics and the diasporic dilemma. *GLQ*, 2, 425–38.

Marshall, T. H. 1950: *Citizenship and Social Class*. Cambridge: Cambridge University Press (reprinted 1973).

Martin, Biddy 1994: Extraordinary homosexuals and the fear of being ordinary. *differences*, 6, 100–25.

Massey, Doreen 1995: Space/power, identity/difference: tensions in the city. In Andy Merrifield and Erik Swyngedouw (eds), *The Urbanization of Injustice*, London: Lawrence and Wishart, 100–16.

Miller, Toby 1993: *The Well-Tempered Self: citizenship, culture, and the postmodern subject*. Baltimore, MD: Johns Hopkins University Press.

Minkowitz, Donna 1997: High anxiety: I was a Stepford queer at the Inaugural Ball. In Amy Gluckman and Betsy Reed (eds), *Homo Economics: capitalism, community, and lesbian and gay life*, New York: Routledge, 21–4.

Moran, Leslie 1991: The uses of homosexuality: homosexuality for national security. *International Journal of the Sociology of Law*, 19, 149–70.

—— 1996: *The Homosexual(ity) of Law*. London: Routledge.

—— 1999: Law made flesh: homosexual acts. *Body & Society*, 5, 39–55.

Morton, Donald (ed.) (1996) *The Material Queer: a lesbigay cultural studies reader*. Boulder, CO: Westview.

Mouffe, Chantal 1993: *The Return of the Political*. London: Verso.

Muñoz, José 1996: Ghosts of public sex: utopian longings, queer memories. In Dangerous Bedfellows (eds), *Policing Public Sex: queer politics and the future of AIDS activism*, Boston, MA: South End Press, 355–72.

Munt, Sally 1995: The lesbian *flâneur*. In David Bell and Gill Valentine (eds), *Mapping Desire: geographies of sexualities*. London: Routledge, 114–25.

—— 1998: Sisters in exile: the Lesbian Nation. In Rosa Ainley (ed.), *New Frontiers of Space, Bodies and Gender*, London: Routledge, 3–19.

Nardi, Peter 1992: That's what friends are for: friends as family in the gay and lesbian community. In Ken Plummer (ed.), *Modern Homo-*

sexualities: fragments of lesbian and gay experience, London: Routledge, 108–20.

O'Donovan, Katherine 1993: Marriage: a sacred or profane love machine? *Feminist Legal Studies*, 1, 75–90.

Oswell, David 1998: True love in queer times: romance, suburbia and masculinity. In Lynne Pearce and Gina Wisker (eds), *Fatal Attractions: rescripting romance in contemporary literature and film*, London: Pluto Press, 157–73.

Pakulski, Jan 1997: Cultural citizenship. *Citizenship Studies*, 1, 73–86.

Palmer, Anya 1995: Lesbian and gay rights campaigning: a report from the coalface. In Angelia Wilson (ed.), *A Simple Matter of Justice? theorizing lesbian and gay politics*, London: Cassell, 32–50.

Parker, Andrew 1993: Unthinking sex: Marx, Engels, and the scene of writing. In Michael Warner (ed.), *Fear of a Queer Planet: queer politics and social theory*, Minneapolis: University of Minnesota Press, 19–41.

Patton, Cindy 1995: Refiguring social space. In Linda Nicholson and Steven Seidman (eds), *Social Postmodernism: beyond identity politics*, Cambridge: Cambridge University Press, 216–49.

—— 1999: 'On me not in me': locating affect in nationalism after AIDS. In Mike Featherstone (ed.), *Love and Eroticism*, London: Sage, 355–74.

Pearce, Lynne and Stacey, Jackie (eds) 1995: *Romance Revisited*. London: Lawrence and Wishart.

Pendleton, Eva 1996: Domesticating partnerships. In Dangerous Bedfellows (eds), *Policing Public Sex: queer politics and the future of AIDS activism*, Boston, MA: South End Press, 373–93.

Phelan, Shane 1994: *Getting Specific: postmodern lesbian politics*. Minneapolis: University of Minnesota Press.

Phillips, Adam 1996: *Monogamy*. London: Faber and Faber.

Phillips, Anne 1993: *Democracy and Difference*. Cambridge: Polity Press.

Plummer, Ken 1995: *Telling Sexual Stories: power, change and social worlds*. London: Routledge.

Probyn, Elspeth 1996: *Outside Belongings*. London: Routledge.

—— 1998: *Mc*-Identities: food and the familial citizen. *Theory, Culture and Society*, 15, 155–73.

Rauhofer, Judith 1998: The possibility of a registered partnership under German law. In Leslie Moran, Daniel Monk and Sarah Beresford (eds), *Legal Queeries: lesbian, gay and transgender legal studies*, London: Cassell, 68–80.

Richardson, Diane 1996: Heterosexuality and social theory. In Diane Richardson (ed.), *Theorising Heterosexuality: telling it straight*, Buckingham: Open University Press, 1–20.

—— 1998: Sexuality and citizenship. *Sociology*, 32, 83–100.

Roche, Maurice 1992: *Rethinking Citizenship: welfare, ideology and change in modern society*. Cambridge: Polity Press.

Rosario, Vernon (ed.) 1997: *Science and Homosexualities*. New York: Routledge.

Rubin, Gayle 1993: Thinking sex: notes for a radical theory of the politics of sexuality. In Henry Abelove, Michele A. Barale and David M. Halperin (eds), *The Lesbian and Gay Studies Reader*, London: Routledge, 3–44.

—— 1998: The miracle mile: South of Market and gay male leather, 1962–1997. In James Brook, Chris Carlsson, and Nancy J. Peters (eds), *Reclaiming San Francisco: history, politics, culture*, San Francisco, CA: City Lights Books, 247–72.

Sedgwick, Eve Kosofsky 1985: *Between Men: English literature and male homosocial desire*. New York: Columbia University Press.

—— 1990: *Epistemology of the Closet*. Berkeley: University of California Press.

—— 1998: A dialogue on love. *Critical Inquiry*, 24, 611–31.

Seidman, Steven 1991: *Romantic Longings: love in America, 1830–1980*. New York: Routledge.

—— 1992: *Embattled Eros: sexual politics and ethics in contemporary America*. New York: Routledge.

—— 1998: Are we all in the closet? Notes towards a sociological and cultural turn in queer theory. *European Journal of Cultural Studies*, 1, 177–92.

Seidman, Steven and Nicholson, Linda (eds) 1995: *Social Postmodernism: beyond identity politics*. Cambridge, Cambridge University Press.

Serlin, David 1996: The twilight (zone) of commercial sex. In Dangerous Bedfellows (eds), *Policing Public Sex: queer politics and the future of AIDS activism*, Boston, MA: South End Press, 45–52.

Sibley, David 1995: *Geographies of Exclusion: society and difference in the west*. London: Routledge.

Signorile, Michelangelo 1993: *Queer in America: sex, the media and the closets of power*. New York: Random House.

Sinfield, Alan 1996: Diaspora and hybridity: queer identities and the ethnicity model. *Textual Practice*, 10, 271–93.

—— 1998: *Gay and After*. London: Serpent's Tail.

Singer, Linda 1993: *Erotic Welfare: sexual theory and politics in the age of epidemic*. New York: Routledge.

Smith, Anna Marie 1994: *New Right Discourse on Race and Sexuality: Britain 1968–1990*. Cambridge: Cambridge University Press.

—— 1997: The centring of right-wing extremism through the construction of an 'inclusionary' homophobia and racism. In Shane Phelan (ed.), *Playing with Fire: queer politics, queer theories*, New York: Routledge, 113–38.

Smith, Barbara 1993: Homophobia: why bring it up? In Henry Abelove, Michele A. Barale and David M. Halperin (eds), *The Lesbian and Gay Studies Reader*, London: Routledge, 99–102.

—— 1997: Where has gay liberation gone? An interview with Barbara Smith. In Amy Gluckman and Betsy Reed (eds), *Homo Economics: capitalism, community, and lesbian and gay life*, London: Routledge, 195–207.

Smyth, Cherry (ed.) 1992: *Lesbians Talk Queer Notions*. London: Scarlet Press.

Soysal, Yasemin 1994: *Limits of Citizenship: migrants and postnational membership in Europe*. Chicago: University of Chicago Press.

Sparks, Holloway 1997: Dissident citizenship: democratic theory, political courage, and activist women. *Hypatia*, 12, 74–110.

Squires, Judith 1994: Private lives, secluded places: privacy as political possibility. *Environment and Planning D: Society and Space*, 12, 387–401.

Stacey, Jackie and Pearce, Lynne 1995: The heart of the matter: feminists revisit romance. In Lynne Pearce and Jackie Stacey (eds), *Romance Revisited*, London: Lawrence and Wishart, 11–45.

Stacey, Judith 1998: Families against 'The Family'. *Radical Philosophy*, 89, 2–7.

Stychin, Carl 1995: *Law's Desire: sexuality and the limits of justice*. London: Routledge.

—— 1996: To take him 'at his word': theorizing law, sexuality and the US military exclusion policy. *Social and Legal Studies*, 5, 179–200.

—— 1998: *A Nation By Rights: national cultures, sexual identity politics, and the discourse of rights*. Philadelphia, PA: Temple University Press.

Sullivan, Andrew 1996: *Virtually Normal: an argument about homosexuality*. London: Picador.

Tatchell, Peter 1992: *Europe in the Pink: lesbian and gay equality in the new Europe*. London: Gay Men's Press.

—— 1996: It's just a phase: why homosexuality is doomed. In Mark Simpson (ed.), *Anti-Gay*, London: Cassell, 35–54.

—— 1998: Battered, bewildered and betrayed. *Gay Times*, April, 17–18.

Taylor, Ian, Evans, Karen and Fraser, Penny 1996: *A Tale of Two Cities: global change, local feeling and everyday life in the North of England*. London: Routledge.

Thrift, Nigel (2000) Not a straight line, but a curve; or, cities are not mirrors of modernity. In David Bell and Azzedine Haddour (eds), *City Visions*, Harlow: Prentice-Hall, 233–63.

Turner, Bryan 1990: Outline of a theory of citizenship. *Sociology*, 24, 187–214.

——(ed.) 1993: *Citizenship and Social Theory*. London: Sage.

Valentine, Gill 1993: Negotiating and managing multiple sexual identities: lesbian time-space strategies. *Transactions of the Institute of British Geographers*, 18, 237–48.

Van Every, Jo 1992: Who is the 'family'? The assumptions of British social policy. *Critical Social Policy*, 33, 62–75.

Waaldijk, Kees and Chapman, Andrew (eds) 1993: *Homosexuality: a European Community issue*. Dordrecht: Martinus Nijhoff.

Warner, Michael 1993: Introduction. In Michael Warner (ed.), *Fear of a Queer Planet: queer politics and social theory*, Minneapolis: University of Minnesota Press, vii–xxxi.

——(ed.) 1993: *Fear of a Queer Planet: queer politics and social theory*. Minneapolis: University of Minnesota Press.

——1999: *The Trouble with Normal: sex, politics, and ethics in queer life*. New York: Free Press.

Watney, Simon 1995: AIDS and the politics of queer diaspora. In Monica Dorenkamp and Richard Henke (eds), *Negotiating Lesbian and Gay Subjects*, New York: Routledge, 53–70.

Weeks, Jeffrey 1977: *Coming Out: homosexual politics in Britain, from the nineteenth century to the present*. London: Quartet Books.

——1990: *Coming Out: homosexual politics in Britain from the nineteenth century to the present*. London: Quartet Books (revised and updated edition).

——1991: *Against Nature: essays on history, sexuality and identity*. London: Rivers Oram.

——1995: *Invented Moralities: sexual values in an age of uncertainty*. Cambridge: Polity Press.

——1997: The delicate web of subversion, community, friendship, and love (Jeffrey Weeks in conversation with Sue Golding). In Sue Golding (ed.), *The Eight Technologies of Otherness*, London: Routledge, 320–33.

——1999: The sexual citizen. In Mike Featherstone (ed.), *Love and Eroticism*, London: Sage, 35–52.

Weir, John 1996: Going in. In Mark Simpson (ed.), *Anti-Gay*, London: Cassell, 26–34.

Weston, Kath 1995: Get thee to a big city: sexual imaginary and the great gay migration. *GLQ*, 2, 253–77.

——1998: Families we choose. In Peter Nardi and Beth Schneider (eds), *Social Perspectives in Lesbian and Gay Studies*, London: Routledge, 390–411.

White, Edmund 1980: *States of Desire: travels in gay America*. London: André Deutsch.

Whittle, Stephen 1998: *Gemeinschaftsfremden* – or how to be shafted by your friends: sterilization requirements and legal staus recognition for the transsexual. In Leslie Moran, Daniel Monk and Sarah Beresford (eds), *Legal Queeries: lesbian, gay and transgender legal studies*, London: Cassell, 42–56.

Williams, Fiona 1992: *Social Policy: a critical introduction*: Cambridge: Polity Press.

Wilson, Angelia 1995: Introduction. In Angelia Wilson (ed.), *A Simple Matter of Justice?: theorizing lesbian and gay politics*, London: Cassell, 1–9.

Wilson, Elizabeth 1993: Is transgression transgressive? In Joseph Bristow and Angelia Wilson (eds), *Activating Theory: lesbian, gay, bisexual politics*, London: Lawrence and Wishart, 107–17.

Wolfson, Evan 1996: Why we should fight for the freedom to marry: the challenges and opportunities that will follow a win in Hawaii. *Journal of Gay, Lesbian, and Bisexual Identity*, 1, 79–89.

Woods, Gregory 1998: *A History of Gay Male Literature: the male tradition*. New Haven, CT: Yale University Press.

Yeatman, Anna 1994: *Postmodern Revisionings of the Political*. New York: Routledge.

Yingling, Thomas 1991: AIDS in America: postmodern governance, identity, and experience. In Diana Fuss (ed.), *Inside/Out: lesbian theories, gay theories*, New York: Routledge, 291–310.

Young, Iris Marion 1989: Polity and group difference: a critique of the ideal of universal citizenship. *Ethics*, 99, 250–74.

—— 1990: *Justice and the Politics of Difference*. Princeton, NJ: Princeton University Press.

—— 1997: Unruly categories: a critique of Nancy Fraser's dual systems theory. *New Left Review*, 222, 147–60.

Žižek, Slavoj 1997: Multiculturalism, or, the cultural logic of multi-national capitalism. *New Left Review*, 225, 28–52.

Index

Compiled by Meg Davies (Registered Indexer, Society of Indexers)